MANIMAL WOE

ARROWSMITH
PRESS

MANIMAL WOE
Fanny Howe

Boston — New York — San Francisco — Baghdad
San Juan — Kyiv — Istanbul — Santiago, Chile
Beijing — Paris — London — Cairo — Madrid
Milan — Melbourne — Jerusalem — Darfur

11 Chestnut St.
Medford, MA 02155

arrowsmithpress@gmail.com
www.arrowsmithpress.com

ISBN: 978-1-7346416-5-3

Design: Purtill Family Business
Cover: Taylor Davis, *And I Turned Myself*, 2020, watercolor and gouache on paper, 22 ½ × 30 inches
Illustrations: Colleen McCallion
Back cover: Photograph by Helen Howe Braider

MANIMAL WOE

WOE

Fanny Howe

He who knows how to grant comfort becomes the guarantor of hope, the keeper of one's image of oneself…No ideals of self-sacrifice or courage are now at work. Just the inner necessity to defend what has become too precious to be destroyed.

—Ilona Karmel, *Keepers of the Image*

Dear Daddy,

Don't worry. I know you're dead.

It's been nearly seven decades. Today is sweltering hot, 100 degrees, and already in July the leaves are drained of early green and swing heavily on the branches.

Often it seems that measurements between things are illusory. Objects are donations given by invisible entities to our daily lives.

One reason death is so perplexing is that it's not what you think it is. Death comes before the wind stops blowing.

Levels of perception are infinite. One perception leads to another.
Every one of them is linguistic, poetic. The sun, for one.

Life folds over, or turns another way.
No wonder we are so estranged from each other.

Laborers are unrewarded artists
We learn the math with our hands and no names.

Your letters to me have been mailed from a library 3,000 miles away and 63 years after you wrote them.

I'm using them as a way to go forward now.

I have a short time to fulfill this task. The branches that swing and nod outside the window are old elms and chestnuts beside Tory houses, and slate pavements, messy nuts in shells and berries waxy red.

It was always hard for me to leave home, not because of family but because of the trees, bushes, robins, cardinals, yellow leaves, chipmunks, rabbits, lilacs, and other wildlife. These were abundant in Mount Auburn cemetery where I played and now walk.

"There's still not a drop of rain in these parts, there hasn't been more than a five minute's gentle shower since you left Cambridge."

Dreams of your return assure me I will recognize you when you come. I think a dream is the resurrection of forgotten things, in Urdu it is too. Visualize your dream figures and you will discover them at an outpost. We arrived at Back Bay Station this time.

In Boston Common, men gathered in protest, and a homeless worker shouted words from Psalms:

"Hypocrites! Malice! Oppressors! Slander!"

In the 1950s, everyone was talking about Joseph McCarthy around the house, the streets, at school. He was a Senator who used fascist techniques to shame, humiliate, and send into social exile anyone who had been affiliated with communists. He stirred up a huge part of the American population (only a few years after Hitler) to hate and fear anything he called un-American. He sought out some who were infiltrating the sciences, those that had military ties especially. He succeeded in destroying careers in Hollywood as well as in colleges and the military.

McCarthy was a drunk who didn't like women much. He was anti-intellectual, belligerent. Roy Cohn was his assistant.

In 1952 Senator William E. Jenner of Indiana (and head of the Communist-hunting Jenner Committee) called three Harvard professors "Pink Boys."

"Why they hate America so much, I don't know," said Jenner, and named Arthur M. Schlesinger Jr., Francis Lee Higgenson, and Mark DeWolfe Howe as those three Pink Boys.

But McCarthy was implicated in the Lavender conspiracy against homosexuals. His tactics were copied by several Republicans thereafter.

Sea-faring men from Bristol, Rhode Island, the DeWolfes were mad slave-traders. All people are wicked, but not all organize their wickedness into financial profit. To keep "DeWolfe" was also to confess your sinful place in American history, not to hide from it. Plantations and concentration camps aren't the same; neither are brothels and orphanages; but they stay in one place unlike trains and ships at sea that can hide their cargo then throw some of it into darkness to be eaten. Little did the slavers know that they were carrying over music, poetry, prayer, gospel, dance, resilience, healthcare, public speaking, athletics, story-telling, created over years and centuries of relations close to universal laws.

Now the chicken is the cow of the world.

The name you get at birth determines too much.

I never liked adults; they came as they were.

One night we sat on the screened porch. It was September and Ma's garden below was already disheveled and downward turning. Peonies lay their heads on daisies, mums on lavender, sweet peas on roses.

To conclude a conversation we were having about segregation (or was it integration?) in Boston, you said this:

"Liberty and equality. Are incompatible. This is the first contradiction you need to know. It describes the fault line in America and in its Constitution."

Had to think about this. Always perplexed by paradoxes, impossibilities, religious matters: was there a trick? If you only knew how many books I have read on theology and philosophy, then you might understand my confusion and poor decision-making.

"Liberty is for the owners. Equality, the masses, or slaves. The troubling underbelly of these concepts is that most labor is equally and inherently unjust. A version of the plantation and prison. And I am not just talking about women, prostitution, cleaning services."

Did anyone in your house believe in God?

Ours was an atheistic and aesthetic household. Thoughts were little gods that had fallen, like puffs of wind, from the night sky. Thought was outside law, and not even quite language. We had to pull at it. I prefer it to all other activity in my body. Thought studies what does not exist, and it's quiet about what does.

But we aren't speaking of these abstractions.

You mean? That law like language refers to itself?

No. Life is the enemy of the law. Law struggles to prevent something new from living.

Daddy, let me ask you this. What is the meaning of life?

"Spare time."

In 2020 my interviewer asked:

Were your father and Alger Hiss close?

It depends on how you mean close. They were friends, not co-conspirators.

Was your father affectionate?

Pa and I never physically touched each other throughout the years, not by hand or by cheek. We played fondly with our dogs side by side and took many walks around Fresh Pond together. But never a touch or word of affection. There was still formality between middle class parents and children. You picked up affection by the look in a person's eyes.

My parents rarely touched each other.

The 200 letters he wrote to me in my teens when I was miles up in Maine (1957) or miles and miles away in California were egalitarian. Their attitude triggered my expectations of a better world.

How do you still have the letters? Where were they all that time?

I swear I don't know how they survived. It mystifies me that I moved houses so often, without taking much, once the children had left home, and still his letters to me survived in good order. The lettering is distinct. Typed or handwritten. Like figures of people we barely remember. They were inside an ordinary box for children's shoes.

Dear Fan:

A note written in the middle of a hot afternoon of the 4th is likely to be as soggy as its author - so don't expect much. We are just back from a sweltering drive to the waterfront of Boston, so that Sukey might find subjects for drawing. We then crept, irritable and ill-tempered, through a maze of traffic - all angry and depressed. A final effort to give Hellie a pony ride failed - the ponies were wisely refusing to come out in the heat. And last night there was the usual pilgrimage to Cambridge Common to see the fireworks - much more pleasantly observable, as I've discovered too late from our own windows. So if you feel dreary - as perhaps you do - remember that all would not have been cheer and rosiness at 58. I'm afraid it's the old story - life and affection are demanding and often frustrating.

An elliptical prose style, not devious but cautious; as if backward-turning to gesture forward.

I am using writing to show portions of a history that we shared and that took place at the level of protest against power: weak, barely heard but untiring.

> Writing seems like a timid approximation of thought.
> Thoughts are like otherworldly floaters from eternity.
> What happens between the raised pen and the brain?
> Does the day drink the sky at night?

One year I was sent away for the summer to a camp in Maine to learn more French. It was 1957 and my love of the French language and a promise from *mon pere* to send me to Paris the next summer allowed this to happen. I was terrified, but my parents needed me out of the way. He drove me four hours north in July and then he wrote to me every day I was gone.

He felt guilty because a camp is a camp, the rules ruin the time spent obeying them, eating and sleeping on command is oppressive.

Guilt from the War years when he wrote of his regret at not being home with me and my sister when we were very young. 1957 was the year the Voting Rights Act was passed, voting was what he called "the most important area in which discrimination can have damaging effects."

We talked politics on the drive to Colby College, and stopped at a Howard Johnson's for lunch and overheard people speaking French. With that language, my imminent separation from home, from him, grew grave and fearful. I was sixteen but an infant. Lyrical thinking patterns, muffled rhythms, weathers, bells that rang across Sundays, thought as a form of music you can't turn off — this was the education I received in Maine. With my uncle's footlocker and Baudelaire in hand.

Chère Fan:

Encore je me trouble quand je pense de le trunc de ton oncle. C'est terrible, ce que je tu demands - mais, comme en dit en Amerique, "that's life." Hier ta soeur Suki "came down" (comme en dit aux Etats-Unis) avec le "twenty-four hour" grippe. Tu peux imaginer quelle "frenzy" (comme en dit à Boston) swept la maison; la pauvre fille croit que le vomit se viendra de moment à moment - mais jamais de "throw-up" (au langage de Cambridge) ou de "up-chuck" (comme dissent les gamains) a se jetter dans le pot ou elsewhere. Aujourdui elle rest à la maison, mais la temperature est normale. Ta Maman, comme tu peux imaginer, était dans un grand "tail-spin," mais le ciel est plus bright ce matin. J'èspaire que c'est le meme chose au Villedeaux, Maine. There's no other news on this front. Cambridge is still as dry as a bone - all the grass is yellow and hay fever is about three weeks ahead of time.

I never really knew the difference between parables, stories, fables, and days: I would "read the signs." So why was I always planning to leave, since the age of fourteen until today? What pathology made it difficult for me to stay anywhere? I kept coming back to Boston—no, Cambridge—and then leaving as fast as I could.

I guess you preferred freedom at any cost.

I'm just afraid of adults, and Boston represents parents to me.

"The weather continues to be frantically bad—northeasters, cold, and wind—"

Human and animal bones fester under our feet, wherever we walk. Like crabs they snap at us to keep us moving.

The figure in your photo is solitary but in motion like a species of insect with attributes and desires so delicate and without force that few notice it.

Like the initials FQH shivering on a white page, all that's left are loaves of open papers for the birds.

When, as if swollen with water, my cells enlarge and I can feel what I know
I feel.
It's like... not pleasure, but a drive.

I know where I'm going but the Lord knows who I'll marry.

My mother sang this. It went on:

Some say he's black and some say he's bonny.
But the fairest of them all is my handsome, winsome Johnny.

18

There must be a reason not to kill anyone who gets in your way.
There must be a secret value each person has. Outside of the military.

Why? Why must there be? What value? For whom?

I suppose natural laws were supposed to insure there were a few creatures left to protect in case we needed them.
The assumption, even behind the Commandments, suggests that humans are only valuable in relation to others, and then very rarely. The continuing anxiety about family ties —

Is it true that authorities fear their workers and at the same time demand that the workers protect them?

Yes, this is true, it happens.

Alien labor is what you are describing. As old as prostitution. People want strangers in the fields, their beds, and factories, and will pay them to hide their eyes from God and keep away.
They don't want to see or know them. Like the old and the insane, discards.

This is how slaves stay alive and anonymous.

Will anyone miss the workers when soft robots take over?
The work they once did will miss them.

Do you believe that wage labor is slave labor when the workers do not get a share of the profit?

Of course. But this is an outdated language that goes all the way back to Someone. She sees that the laborer is given useless, killing work, and is unable to use their imagination to learn intelligent lessons from their hands and tools. For her, there is first the physical work itself, then there is what it tells us about the laws of nature, stars, the void, and the most important lesson is to show young people how to see God in everything.

Talk about old-fashioned.

Really?

Well, I would break with her religious views.

And leave only birth and death. Only those two. Surprises.

What I hate is when people use a worn out vocabulary to keep the old days
        in place.
Holy is one of those words.

To me the word "personal" is the only one I can find to describe my feelings
towards God and others, towards nature, towards days, towards experience
generally, and towards the open-air. I can't call the whole field of feelings
"spiritual" though many do. Many call religious feelings "spiritual" but I'm
going to call them "personal."

        For today anyway. Yesterday the word was "natural." Tomorrow it
might be "intimate."

I came upon this note left by my father:

"Perhaps I should state my theological position at the outset — What
Time has described as a 'non-denominational' Christian — What the
Fund for the Republic calls a 'humanist' — what others might call a
secularist or an Atheist."

Who are you talking to out the window there? Would you like a bit more tea?

Not now. Thanks. It's raining.

You wanted to speak about your father.

Years after he disappeared, I am trying to trace the unfolding of his life and time. And two things more — not so simple — I want to think about his pursuits, and to know that he died when his work was complete and he could do no more.

I don't believe you. Is there a time when a person's life is complete?

I think there are signs given to you when your life in history is complete. A doubling of doubt, then regret. Heart failure, a stroke... To realize that your work was more dream than life.

> Your dreams are alive. Like your thoughts.
> There is nothing that isn't alive.
> How do we know if we have finished what we planned to do?
> Noticing that old, even dead, figures and ideas return.

What?

I'm not a lawyer. I am taking the theory of recapitulation as my guide.

What's that?

Recapitulation is backward thinking, like the composition of a poem or song. You look across a finished thing in order to understand it. You have to go over it again, but include your presence this time. You are now part of the thing you are going over. You can't ever escape this problem of being where you are as a negative presence. You write facts backwards and forwards and repeat some of it between trying to get yourself out of it. It's like recycling but reinventing at the same time. In the process of recapitulating, you readjust your impressions of an earlier outcome and shift them a little. I wonder why this is so hard to say.

It sounds like testing to see if anything ever happened at all!

Did it?

We were in the late 20th century archiving and reassessing people's work.

That's still happening.

When did your father begin to notice inequality?

The usual way.

What's that?

At home. In his own city, body, siblings.

Okay, so give us the beginning — the night he died.

Where he went that night, and what, historically, that time and year meant to the country, was (I see now) weirdly fitting. A person of his time and type would no longer be useful to the movements after 1968. Or only in a referential way, because his teaching did reverberate. When you trace some letters and talks he gave, you can see the archetypal teacher who stands at our shoulders while we read the paper. His ideas can clarify the thoughts we breeze through now. Actually this is because of the lyric, the song that continues under everything. I can hear Simone Weil in Giorgio Agamben, even if he can't.

What did you hear behind your father's words?

You really want to know? The night he died, he had attended a meeting in Roxbury about school busing, although he was already feeling some pain in his chest. It was a cold February night. He had shoveled snow, and when the call came to where I lived, I wasn't surprised by the news. I had been dreaming that he was dying. I will say that this coincidence increased my belief in a hidden order. An implicate order.

The year was 1967, and the unofficial conclusion of the civil rights movement would soon end in bloodshed, assassination, and Vietnam. The kind of "white liberal" he represented was on its way out.

So were the Stealthy Wealthy, the old-time philanthropists.

Shortly before his death, at a meeting of lawyers on civil rights, one of them wondered aloud why Blacks were so repelled by Whites. "Because we're frauds," my father said, "and they know it."

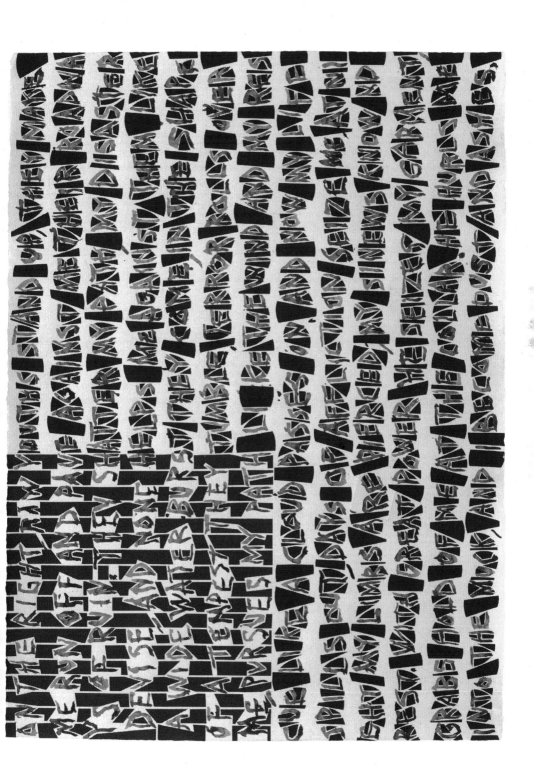

There seem to be contradictions everywhere. "For instance, negative liberty is a liberty free of obstacles." Why call it negative? Negative usually means bad. "Free of obstacles" sounds good. Less is more? I don't get it.

Negative as in absent. And present. Somewhere else.

What about rights? Rights are immunities, they exist to restrain human urges. A right is protective, not a demand. Rights also suggest that others are enemies. When you cry out for a right, you are claiming that you deserve what you want. That life itself is imposing unfair limits on a person. Do children have rights? Not that they know of. There are no rights when it comes to death. We all have to agree that something did happen before us. We have objects to prove it, to agree on.

For instance many decades ago in America there were those who took advantage of post-War fever and leftover hate to make trouble for anyone in this country who was not "a patriot," a blank slate White person. It's unclear how much ignominy anyone believed. But they did a good job of pretending, and turned on many institutions, not just people, to stake out their traitors. McCarthy called Harvard the "Kremlin on the Charles."

What McCarthy would do became a question of what Harvard would do, and then what my father and some of his friends would do. In this case, Harvard did not dismiss the accused professors (called by McCarthy "Fifth Amendment Communists") and (honestly) various colleagues stated that the accused were being stubborn in their own defense and should just clear out.

I think the Republicans were beginning to evolve into enemies already. The Psalms refer to such enemies often.

So my father wrote his letters to several senators, repeating his position that McCarthy was a far greater danger to the country than the people he was accusing of being Communists. The contempt that McCarthy and his Senate committees had for law was a way of "overthrowing the government," so what was democracy good for if no one seemed to perceive this paradox and take action? I asked him questions and always got answers, never silence. But plot can only be understood retroactively, and by the time a story is understood, most of the questions that were important earlier have been folded over into another. There is no way to separate the venom of McCarthyism from the coming war against Civil Rights.

What's the time?

The word "time" is a good marker for changing the subject. Give me some background.

He was born in 1906. He had a brother and a sister and a mother and father. He was lucky. He was loved.

What can you see as the truest figure, the most legible, of this person, your father?

I suppose it is the person on paper. First, during the War he sent us V-letters on thin blue paper. Then, when my mother returned to Ireland in 1936, a year after their marriage, his opinions in his letters to her were caustic and idealistic at the same time.

She threw papers away but kept these letters.

1935

Dear Mol,

I become more and more depressed by Boston. The hopeless stuffiness of everyone - their snug satisfaction with their assumed security, and their irritation with me all stir my blood up. What is there that has killed this community so completely dead. It isn't only that I see a limited group - I have tried to find another world in Civil Liberties - but there the only vitality takes a Ford Hall form of jolliness. The brains on State Street, which still exist, have withdrawn into their own intricacies and jealousies, and the body of the community has been stifled by Catholicism.

I really began to think that Communists are right in calling all Republicans - and particularly big-business Republicans - Fascists when these nice leading citizens, one an ex-governor of Maine, began discussing the best means of depriving the uneducated and unemployed of their voice. The one essential which they agreed upon was that anyone receiving WPA relief should be disenfranchised, and they likewise believed such a step constitutional.

An evening of a Tavern dinner - at which in sullen silence my temperature, during political discussion, surged to a new high, and during which I sat in silence, for which now I am totally ashamed. First, President Lowell (the murderer of Sacco and Vanzetti) and I sat chatting, or rather screaming, at each other on educational topics. Then gradually the Landon forces began to gather - rugged, rock-ribbed men all of them. Slowly the smoke of hatred began to slip from their aristocratic nostrils, and finally Roosevelt was strapped to the burning pyre of anger.

To my shame I sat in silence - but I literally was too shocked and horrified to hear such suggestions from the lips of respectable, and intelligent men to say anything. These are the people whom democracy has favored, and they are the first to turn upon it and seek means for its destruction. The only satisfaction which I got from the evening was, first an insight into the real mentality of conservatism, and, second, a new indignation with my own class.

28

July 28, 1957

Dear Fan:

    Many thanks for your letter which arrived this morning. These are sure to be the hardest days and nights - and all who cross your path are likely to take on the quality of creeps. Creeps, however, change their spots with time and I like to think that your healthy resolve to work hard will do more than anything else to improve the prospects. If you can give us more data about your room-mate it would be welcome. Whence comes this character - what age - what charm - what kind of nocturnal noises does she make?

    I'm sorry that the cash I left in your hands was so quickly exhausted in books etc. I take it that if I put a special delivery stamp on this letter it will reach you before the end of the weekend and may give you a temporary feeling of freedom. The Cambridge heat is appalling today, but there's some hope of thunder if not tornadoes by night time. Our gloomy plans still take us to Vineyard Haven tomorrow morning - returning Sunday evening.

    You must now feel that the summer is about over, as it really is.

    It's always a shock to find that the heart of summer has gone when we move into August.

    Lots of love - Pa

We talked often at home about money and homework and movies and political positions. At a speed of 35 miles an hour, the folk revival and Motown played in the car. Late-bloomers as a rule, no one before or after this family made any money.

Daddy, beside me on my left at the end of the bench, in 1965 took me out of school to witness *The Naked Lunch* obscenity trial in Boston. *Motel... Motel...Motel...broken neon arabesque...loneliness moans across the continent.* Riveting how men were so confident, fearless even, Mailer and Ginsberg, imbued with a sense of ownership, of a camaraderie among themselves that must have been learned early.

Now I wonder if class war begins when members of the ruling class grow tired of rules. My father, when young, had contempt for the rich, the comfortable, the segregationists, the management class. They were the ones with the "silence" that was cold and adult until it suddenly broke. They were mobilizing into an anti-democratic bloc around voting rights and what it means to be American. Then I see that I live under White Rule.

My sense is that he was close to forming a general theory of law in these years. He used philosophy and Dickens, Hegel and Holmes as mentors.
He wrote an essay on The Common Law.

Was this after he was the secretary to Oliver Wendell Holmes in DC?

Many years, yes. His journals and letters from the Holmes time are personal, intimate and funny. He was lost and lonely in Washington, and spent his entire year there reading murder mysteries aloud to the great Justice, wiping the old man's bottom, or studying the history of constitutional law. Experience, he learned from Holmes, far out-ranked education. But he was put to work as a teacher and scholar, whether he liked it or not. Holmes' influence would become a burden, the way teachers often do, and then became foundational.

How do you mean?

He was given the heavy load of editing Holmes' letters and writing his biography. It was an interminable task, performed to gratify Felix Frankfurter, who chose him, as Uncle Sam chose men to serve abroad. The job plagued his life. But his fascination with Holmes — and what he learned from the Justice's rebelliousness — lasted.

Why did Frankfurter select him? Selection can be a curse, you know.

I suppose the families Howe and Holmes were similar in many ways. Patrician 19th century fathers and their 20th century sons who went to war. But Frankfurter must also have seen a style of writing he thought would be compatible with Holmes.

Just tell me a little about those similarities. I really don't know.

They came from the same social background, very particular to Ancient Boston. Because, forever second to New York in terms of power, money, and imagination, Boston held onto its Anglo-status and developed into a city of ethnic neighborhoods, all of them deemed inferior to the WASP bankers and lawyers on State Street. Remains of a British class system. Pet names for the marginalized: wop, bum, jap, jerry, mick, spick, frog, and fairy.

Quite a litany. This is gone now, we hope.

No. As far as I can tell, things never go away, they fade into financial values: architecture, urban blocks, parks, the arts, especially the banks. Tones of voice, jokes. There is a new class in America that could be called the political-critical class.

Maybe. . . Anyway, say about your father's parents.

Well, it's like what I just said. The people who lived on Beacon Hill — Putnams, Lees, Cabots, Paines, Curtises, Coolidges, Codmans, and Lowells. These old folks evolved into brass nameplates on their doors: World Peace Foundation, General Theological Library, Massachusetts Society for the Prevention of Cruelty to Children, United Prison Association of Massachusetts, and International Friendship League.

His mother, Fanny Quincy, while known as "a good hostess," was described by her daughter as tending toward "a deeply ingrained agnosticism" and as a person who perceived "the only reality in life as unhappiness — the stretches of happiness between being only parentheses." However, she was also known to be unusually conscious of inequality, of the suffering of those less fortunate than her family, and for being "modest to a fault." She worked in settlement houses in the South End. He was much more influenced by her than by his father. The Quincys were politicians and dissenters, they leaned towards socialism, the longer they lived.

Were they financially secure?

Not really, the Quincys lost their land and money years before. They lived a life of public service and letters, were respectably eccentric, rabidly democratic, not classy, too well acquainted with books and struggle.

From this little microhistory you can see the way old school Liberals evolved.

Soon after Fanny died, my father met my mother of the Irish theater, who was looking for a husband outside of Dublin. She found him.

And he her.

He was desperate to get married.

Like her.

Obviously they couldn't see the disasters coming — the War, the nuclear bomb, the Red Scare, Vietnam — emigrating from Dublin as she did, my mother knew about war, civil wars, and drama, she was always on alert to the political weather. She was not an admirer of American culture, however, and sided with the underdogs, the Irish, and rebel nations. She even admired Stalin for a while and criticized my father when he was overseas in the war for being too hard on the Russians. She was afraid he had become a classic American isolationist and hater. But no, he hadn't. She was raised by a radical Quaker feminist in Dublin, a woman who founded a trade union for laundry workers. Louie Bennett.

Theirs was what was called "a mixed marriage" in those days.

What?

A mixed marriage was one between Boston and Cambridge, between a worldly and commercial household (and "the risks and brutalities which are their accompaniments") — Republicans were money-mad while Democrats "used their advantages for the preservation of a way of life that had its roots in the traditions of scholarship rather than the accidents of power."

My father and mother were "unmixed and mixed" in many fundamental ways when you take into account their different countries, accents, chances, hopes, experiences, but they both loved Chaplin and other comedians, including mimics like his sister Helen who was four-feet-eleven and a stand-up mime.

Boston, even for Henry James, had a rustic pulse that came from the Bay, the fields and farms, a seasonal unrest that kept the citizens in a kind of hesitant wonder, the city lives so close to wilderness, is conservationist and not quite as socially liberated as history suggests. The sea was always close. A maritime and rocky promontory, a city built on dirt swamps. Bostonians have contempt for Boston.

      "The two worlds (Boston and New York) met at many points, of course, and their fusion often came about by other means than mixed marriages, but the children of such marriages grew up, if not with divided loyalties, at least with a division of alternatives."

This "division of alternatives" caused serious ruptures in tribes like WASPs as time went by. Boston in some ways seems most like DC with its hills and rivers, its slums and its ghosts buried in wetlands, landfill, the graves of slaves, and buildings, monuments, museums.

The War?

He was years gone, having served in Italy, Africa and France with the Civil Affairs Detachment, the 2675 Civil Affairs Regiment, Allied Control Commission, the 2678 Civil Affairs Regiment, and the G-5 Section, 6th Army Group. Went to Potsdam, Washington... We got occasional reports.

Letter from North Africa:

Here the day has been not unlike most others, but there were long conferences in the General's office in Germany, with a recently returned economist telling us something of the gloomy prospects ahead. And I confess that they are gloomy. We seem to have embarked on a program which is bound to provide the Germans with a minimum standard of living, committed ourselves to the industrial demilitarization of Germany, and undertaken to our own taxpayers that there will be sufficient industrial exports from Germany to pay for the wheat, medicines, etc. which are imported into Germany to prevent starvation.

When the Russians transferred eastern Germany to Poland they cut off 25% of the food resources of Germany, and they made inevitable the emigration from the new Poland of millions of Germans who don't want to be Poles. The total result of all this is that we can't possibly expect Germany to live on her present resources, we must send a lot of imports into the country to prevent wholesale starvation, and unless we permit the revival of German heavy industry, and the resurrection of that threat to the peace, we cannot possibly refund ourselves for the goods which we send in. The choice will thus have to be made between abandoning our program of demilitarization and paying out millions in US taxes to feed Germans.

In the meanwhile, as you may have noticed in the papers, for humanitarian and commercial motives mixed, the British movement to let German industry get back on its feet is mounting every day. Against this whole background of virtually insoluble riddles, the American public with fury is demanding the immediate demobilization of the Army and the return of all their sons and husbands to the USA - thus weakening enormously our bargaining power vis-a-vis the Russians, French, and British. It looks very much as if all our paper promises and resolutions to play a part in the world were going up in smoke. As I have long anticipated, the American's provincialism and homesickness is much stronger than his sense of global responsibility.

People from Cambridge say to outsiders that they come from Boston because the train station and airport are there. Or are they ashamed of the association with Harvard and privilege? Or are they secretly being protective of Cambridge?

Boston was another whole proposition as you looked across the river to
       its skies.
Heavy with both history and high rise. Red brick and silver credit cards.
Beacon Hill was a step back from commerce, what lasted was what it was
       originally. A kind of red heifer.

Republicans went to Nantucket and the North Shore.
Democrats (and Socialists) went to Cape Cod and Martha's Vineyard.
So many beginnings to outcomes, the post-War isolationism articulated by
       Joseph McCarthy that became an ideology.
The end of Reconstruction started the Republican Party we now know.
       Rutherford Hayes. The loss of Lincoln.

Well, Christianity is now a position, an ideology. It has nothing to do with its original revolutionary roots in apophantikos.

What do you like about Christianity? I mean, what is it?

A beauty-filled vision of reality where there is a quiet that creates a resting place between the one who sees and the one who is seen. The space, called the spirit, is self-contained and keeps braiding itself into lines, dimensions, circles that cross each other and meet and move on while its wind (or Word) whirls with it, and produces thought, and thought produces speech, all of it contributing to the speed of evolution. So every word comes into existence as a sound, then slides back into non-existence. People get depressed by all this coming and going. They grow ill, weak, they die but the mystery survives.

Boston fulfilled its purpose in the 19th century. A city made out of a hill, or three sister hills, Charlestown, Beacon, and Bunker, as those hills were called, right on the Massachusetts Bay, a place where a person could work in peace, and remain a reformer but not a revolutionary.

Hidden injustices were buried in "the dark woods of legal history." For instance, far away from Boston in 1938, a Black family moved into a subdivision outside Chicago occupied entirely by Whites. They moved in anyway, and were greeted by an angry crowd that would go on to force the family out of their home. The father took the homeowners to court to break the "restrictive covenant" that protected segregated areas. *Hansberry v. Lee* (1940) ruled the covenant to be illegal but not unconstitutional. Remember *Raisin in the Sun*? There has been constant backlash in the US against positive change brought by grassroots movements and people of unnoticed social consequence.

Illegal but not unconstitutional: how is this possible?

Lorraine Hansberry:

"Daddy felt that this country was hopeless in its treatment of Negroes. So he became a refugee from America. He bought a house in Polanco, a suburb of Mexico City, and we were planning to move there when he died. I was fourteen at the time."

MDeWH:

"The Fourteenth Amendment was meant to prohibit all state action which supports a caste system. This was the will of the nation reflected in the affirmations of its traditions."

"The greatest brutality of our time is racial inequality," he realized in the fifties. "I wanted to find out how this brutality has been protected and sustained by the courts."

"So I set out to make law an effective instrument for advancing the personal freedoms and human dignities of the American people."

Can a common law change the nature of one nation if it's divided into parts? Law of any kind can only do this if it is viewed as a continuum, not a single act in a singular context. The land and the rivers can do this best.

Cold War anti-Communist traits morphed into race-rage and White contempt and suspicion.

[There was a woman who sued after finding a dead mouse at the bottom of a milk bottle. Who was to blame? The milker of the cow, the company that bottled it, the store that sold it, the woman who drank it and may be lying for profit?]

I have to say that this is making my breathing difficult.

In January, 1943, my father stood by the front door of our house on Park Street in Buffalo and said goodbye, to join British and American units in North Africa, Italy, Sicily, Southern France, England, and, at the War's end, Potsdam and the Pentagon. He was discharged as a Colonel in December, 1945, having received the Distinguished Service Medal and the Legion of Merit. He saluted during the National Anthem at Red Sox games.

But what did he do (later) for the Pentagon? Will we ever know?

You could petition for a Freedom of Information form.

True, but will I?

No. You have these letters from 1944, preferring to close in on his thoughts through his papers instead of personal histories.

4 days & 3 nights - & with one of each still coming - I've been on a train. At first we were traveling in what is called first class where lice, fleas, heat, food from tin cans, & dirt were the steady diet. We then moved up one peg in society into a freight car for 30 men or six horses, but were fortunate in having no horses sharing our sordid floor and only five of us - with all our baggage to wallow with in our luxury.

You can imagine some of the discomforts of such a life - but the experience on the whole has been rewarding. Last night, however, we really thought the game was up when the rickety train got out of control going down a mountain side. For what seemed like an hour, but was probably no more than ten minutes, we roared along at 70 miles an hour with flames leaping from the brakes, Arabs jumping overboard from their posts at the brakes.

It was not reassuring as we hurtled through the moonlight to see forty cars strewn along the embankments, having run into similar trouble a few weeks ago.

Finally, and just as in one of the old Westerns, we came to a gradual halt. I really think I've never been so scared in my life. There's a crowd of British troops on the train besides these officers in my group - they are simply incredible as regards their tea. All assigned to freight cars - with no facilities for cooking they nevertheless manage every day - at least three times, to take enormous wallows in their indispensable stimulus. Their device is to rush up to the engine at every stop and fill great cans with water from the boiler. Anything to drink has been so scarce on the journey that I have even found myself forming in line at the regular intervals.

I suppose it's nothing but crass sentimentality that makes me almost cry with delight when in some outlandish village with an outlandish name we run into a little group of American troops working on the railroads. Their universal quality of friendly equality horrifies the British officers, no less than does the obvious delight with which the other American officer & I rush to these privates. It was like reaching Mecca to walk into a cook shed in one of the stations the other morning and to share with a pair of railroad privates from Texas and Alabama their breakfast of fried egg sandwiches &, for once, coffee. The British officers evidently thought our conduct most unseemly.

Well... That unseemly rasp on the radio was Hitler. On some nights practice air raids. Roosevelt had shockingly died during the war. Truman took over. The atomic bomb blew into our minds and stayed there. The Russians, just recently our allies and friends, became an obsessive focus of hate-fiction and suspicion. Books and magazines finally showed the underbelly of the war, concentration camps, mass graves, children covered in sores and black soot. This was where the world (to me) began. In carbon images of life; in squares.

Holmes said "war is an organized bore."

Many men love struggle, the blowing up of things, the destruction of cities, the shooting down of peasants and soldiers, the pride of wounds, raping women, raping each other, primitive desire released, the death wish. Their mothers sent them proudly off to kill. The Jeeps hopped over the rubble, the broken pottery and glass... the proximity to more men. Many women prefer men — either being one, having one, or acting like one. The man is the exemplar for Western culture: both protector and destroyer.

Pa to Ma (in Ireland):

On the way back across the Common I stopped on the outskirts of a gathering of "bums" who were also talking politics. This talk had so much more wisdom and vitality to it that I eventually ended up by being encouraged. There was, in the group, the most extraordinary enthusiasm of Roosevelt, coupled with real understanding of his limitations. I even begin to think that he will carry Massachusetts and smear the Tavern and State Street gangsters flatter than a grease spot.

As you can see from this little outburst, the political scene is far from dull... The really important struggle that is going on now here is not actually in politics at all, but between the rival labor factions. The conservative American Federation, headed by Green, is trying to stifle the insurgent and increasingly radical group headed by John L. Lewis, who is out, ultimately, to organize all unskilled labor upon an industrial basis. The fights between the two factions, and between Lewis's crowd and big business, promises to be hot and bloody once, ending, we hope, in a victory for Lewis, and, perhaps, in a really intelligent and co-ordinated labor party.

As for my extra-filing job - please don't take it either too hard or seriously. I only do it occasionally and am rather enjoying it when I get the chance to do it. I seem now to be so caught up in regular office work that I have no time for extra effort. After dining with cousin Alice Gould this evening I rushed off to my new post - manager of a bar in the negro belt. It is a strange profession which tosses up such odd jobs as that - and I have got to devote almost all my time for an indefinite period to cleaning up this messy estate - ordering wines, beers, and spirits for poor broken bums to soak in.

One of the clientele tonight was the brother of the deceased bartender - just back from a term in jail - the most horrible wreck of a man I have ever seen. Seven years ago he came over from Ireland to make his way, and hasn't had one job since he landed - chiefly because he has been drunk and had syphilis ever since. Thrown against the background of the pseudo-respectable, ultra-Catholic lawyers who have been handling the family affairs, the whole scene is a rich and horrible one. It is this crude, low-down side of the law that appeals to me.

In September, 1949, a U.S. spy plane flying over Siberia came upon signs of an explosive radioactivity ("Tsar Bomba" was the name of the Russian bomb). Soon after, President Harry S. Truman admitted that the Soviets had the atomic bomb. Among other detailed information, British spies had given the Soviets a blueprint of the "Fat Man" atomic bomb that had been dropped on Nagasaki, Japan, as well as everything the Los Alamos scientists knew about the potential of the hydrogen bomb, a destructive force hundreds of times more powerful than the Hiroshima and Nagasaki atomic bombs.

The Red Scare Era — Russophobia — represented a fear of progress that this country keeps repeating. Slimy scientists multiplied in cartoons and in life, in animation as men with an accent, either German, Russian, or (oddly) a gay-inflected Brit. An American, Robert Oppenheimer, was the face of a guilty scientist that this country loves to reproduce in cartoons. There was a fellow physicist who worked with him, named David Bohm, who was sidelined from his career by the haters of Communism, and in his exile discovered interconnections in quantum activities that took years to be respected by the scientific community. His vision was influenced by facts and an idea. Gentle, depressed, and thorough, he went from lab to lab to test his insights. He was a genius who was friends with Krishnamurti.

I knew a man like him, who was Austrian, a physicist, who came here after the War, and who worked in a weapons lab near Cambridge, Mass. He was a stoop-shouldered and humble man who bent under the burden of his past as he poured Rhine wine into his friends' glasses. He wanted them to understand the work he did in Germany after the War, and the mystical twist that came with quantum physics. But he couldn't explain it to anyone. He and his wife gave crushing hand-grips to the person they were kissing hello and goodbye. Grips of gratitude and helplessness.

"Be attentive to me and hear me. From the sound of the enemy, from the crushing and force of the wicked when they bring mischief down, fear and trembling enter me, and horror envelops me."

So what is God but ether?

Why are you so obsessed with God?

What better thing than being but not-existing? Being able to hide in the dazzle of nothingness.

I suppose. To exist is to be seen by another.

It's true that as long as you are physically visible, you can be selected and measured. The century to come will produce citizens who must destroy every trace of their identity and crawl like soldiers in the trenches. To disappear will be a vocation. To hide from surveillance.

Who will care?

Every rock and tree. The prisoner may be a pebble on a highway, but the pebble is here to stay. Every day the prisoner awakens and feels and moves around, sees a dash of sky and a drop of sun on the floor.

"The main reason to abolish capital punishment is that you might execute the wrong person."

Wow, Daddy, is that where morality begins? In a mistake? What about the principle?

Never argue on principle.

Then on what?

Who is getting the rawest deal. Be on their side.

But that's Christian.

It's in all religions.

When the Puritans and the Pilgrims sailed away from Britain, how much of the English legal system did they bring with them? There was conservative, there was progressive, and then there was the Federal government. A man named Pratt was the first to use the term "racism" in relation to the "Indians" he was building a school for in Indiana. The word emerged in the mid-nineteenth century, a fairly new concept to define the attitudes of Whites towards Blacks. They made race into a science, they made it objective, useful, a justification for oppression. This opinion included making the poor and the earth itself into an object of use.

Well, yes.

Can you answer me this? When O.W. Holmes asked his mother the following question, was he thinking of protection for his servant, or was he thinking of his own needs?

At the end of his last letter from the Sixth Corps in the Civil War to his mother at home in Boston, Holmes asked: "Do you think I could get a place for my nagur boy if I brought him with me?"

Cultures are opened up, and clothes and people exchanged during wars, arms are improved and waste accumulates. But two generations call to each other across a trench in the night. One comes from the East, one from the West, and no matter how wide the trench or how narrow in the night, they cannot explain, one to the other, the furnishings of their loneliness, their experiences, the places they passed through.

The H-bomb. A great equalizer.

The dead or naked body of a Human is as alien as an alien. Los Alamos, Roswell, Boston, and Hiroshima.

If you are given no taste of religion when you are young, you only have a small chance of becoming a believer later. Creatures unfold over time. What was put into them is still there. What is missing will never be there. We are complete in utero and from there we attach new facts but never a new substance. You can, of course, fake your beliefs.

Equality has a measure that is (invisible) universal as a social mark, therefore it doesn't matter except as an idea. But what idea does it serve? Judgment. You are given equality in order to disappear. If you are seen, you are judged. Many legal terms spring out of Equality. It can only be a spiritual word in the end, ironically without measure, like hope and charity. It's not a word that defends the rights of a single person to exist, but describes existence as contingent only on itself. "Hey that's not fair," is how it is expressed by children.

My aunt Helen told me in 1968, "If you marry him, your children will suffer."

Will my grandchildren receive equal protection under the law of the
United States?

Equal to what, to whom?
I will try again: Will all children receive the same amount of protection
in the world?

Equal is not the same as the same.

Either begin with the infant or the dirt. Each one carries its origins into its designated future. One produces wheat, one water.

Someone told me we are all born equal as bodies in existence, nameless, random, until our blood is drawn. Wrong?

The first level of poverty is earth to which we return. Dirt, water, minerals. It's at that level that we live every day, it's this which is meant by "the poorest." We have a contract with our flesh that steams with emotions.

Impossible to make disappear. It is here. From here all else is potential.

I dreamed last night my son was working in the next room and my daughter in a room after that. I walked down the hall to check, re-realizing that I always slept best with a child in the house. A child I could look after.

I once loved a fat man who smelled like ginger snaps.
Now he is ash. We had ginger snaps and a cup of tea.
Nothing came of it.

No cup of tea (or person) ever tastes just like the other.
But ginger snaps are all the same.

"Born equal" means each one has a value in the order. More than value, place. A place in the universal scheme. The same as the others. Impossible to dissolve into a zero or a negative. The down side of this is that a person may continue misperceiving while others are being exterminated.

Born equal before being born. . . you are equal in potential. It has nothing to do with measurement but with movement. These words in this line are almost equal:

A slave, even alive, even alone, I love.

Love is out of place in that line.

People's attachment to the word love is because love is the only emotion that eludes slavery. But love is now one of those tainted words, not useful in our too-bright times. Only in the dark.

45

Saturday, Oct 25 '58?.

Dear Fan:

My faithless pen didn't seem to pour much ink in your direction
during the last week. Why it was so dry I don't know - probably because
there's been the usual emptiness. The one ripple on the surface was
last night when the Russian Ambassador appeared at the Law School Forum
abd spoke (poorly) to a relatively hostile audience which of course,
included resentful Hungarians, etc. I was the so-called Moderator and
had to introduce Menshikov and try to keep things relatively tranquil.
On the whole things went smoothly. Today there's the Harvard-Dartmouth
game to which I was to take Helen - but a Northeaster has settled on
the town and I've disposed of the tickets. Sukey appeared at the Forum
last night with Quinny, Edith, Henry, and Annie Lord - and they were at
the house afterwoards. Sukey seems in fine form. She has made a fuss,
with others, about the bad teaching of painting at the School and it
may be that the protest will bring results. In any case it stirred up
her blood to be in a fight. She reports that she had a good letter from
you containing essentially good news. We'll be glad to hear of the
outcome of exams etm. On Tuesday Mummy and Hnunt Helen and I are
scheduled to head off for Vermont with Aunt Mabel's ashes - there's
some question whether Mummy will be able to shake herself loose from
Grandpa and Hellie - but we hope she can manage it - though the journey
is hardly a very exciting one to make. You'll be impressed to hear
that both Mummy and I have given up smoking - aHd that I really seem,
after the fourth day, to passed over the fatal line. I'm probably about
to become as fat as a butter ball - in which case I'll have to go back
to the weed - but already I think that I can say that I begin to feel
better.

Of such trividdities is life made up. Have you been as yet to
the Film Festival with Herb - or is that later on? All droppings of
gossip are most welcome. What of your writing? What of your sex-life?
And what, I might add, of your spiritual life?

Love from all -

Pa

Try to send me your vacation
dates so that I can try for
reservations.

46

How can you tell hysterical laughter from sobbing? I've never seen it. And now my insights are over. Even laws of nature can be interrupted and cut down like human laws, but there are laws that are secret and we live by them. To make a bell instead of a fruit? I can tell you this. That which is over is everywhere. The Father is over and will never be saved. The Father is over like the Sabbath and the swamis. They noticed that laws are fears, and fears fade away. That law stays, the law of change. The music is over. When you find yourself in the sepulcher you will not feel the transmission you hoped for. Discarded among bones, neither the all or the nothing, you must say, I am finished, in order to release a future into the air.

A limited future, a new view. You have seen the boots of the dead standing at the office door. In all directions, buckles and rubber. Hollows for feet and ankles. Their use is completed. A living embryo contains all of itself (past and future) (health and illness) inside the constraints of its flesh.

MDeWH, a note:

One of the most scandalous aspects of the Constitution as it was then written was that although everyone knew that the central problem was going to be slavery, the Federal Constitution didn't use the word slavery or face the question of what should be done about it. If the nation was unable to abolish it, it was also unable to acknowledge that it existed.

This Nation's commitment to silence on the largest issue that confronted the American people was at once a distinctive and a startling contribution to the art of government. The largest issue was, of course, slavery, and then segregation, in spite of three corrective amendments to the Constitution.

Silence is given to women to use after they have been beaten, verbally beaten, pursued, threatened and lied about. A survival technique. The women who lived with their fathers also were silent.

The way a person writes, not the handwriting but the composition, indicates hidden prejudices and assumptions, and sensitivity to social conventions. Even kindness, even despair. The grammatical structure does what a tone of voice does. But there is no need to deconstruct it once the writer has died. Already it will have thinned out into the next generation's speech patterns, like a cushion too often sat on. Traces of the first voice will linger and in the grammar there will be signs and symptoms of an earlier time in history. But you will already be judging what you read according to your training and education on the streets, you will therefore ruin (or clarify) the intent of the original.

In 1957 City Lights Books in San Francisco published *The White Negro* by Norman Mailer. I have a copy here with my old husband's handwriting in the margins: slanted, pointed, urgent.

"Existentialism: Along comes the American existentialist, the hipster, the one who knows that if our collective condition is to live with instant death by atomic war, relatively quick death by the State, or with a slow death by conformity with every creative and rebellious instinct, then that person must run into their own self and begin life there, where they can die on their own terms."

It's true we all will be victims of death, but according to what I know it will be given to us suddenly, randomly, indifferently. Death does a sudden thing alone.

Until that happens, you have your ideas, your personal, intimate, natural
       thoughts.
This is good. You can live your own life in company or in mortal loneliness.

Something didn't happen to me, but what was it?

In 1957 Congress wrestled with the issue of civil rights. "This is an hour for great moral stamina," said Representative Adam Clayton Powell, Jr., of New York, one of three African-American Members in Congress.

48

He was right. In this country, every law reverts to the subject of race because like love it remains outside the law. I mean, like death.

Fear of Communism is another subject that gives us a hint of the true fear in America.
I was washed down the cement steps of the San Francisco Court House by firefighters protecting the HUAC inside. It was, I believe, 1959. I was sure I knew what a person should be: singular, free.

The oak trees tip towards the north, and their branches seem to fill with tears, even desire. You have to wonder if desire looks like repulsion from another angle. You have to wonder if one anticipates the arrival of another by a shriveling in the outer skin. We are the only creatures that need clothing, Adam, thanks to you. Before, we must have been able to live outdoors, naked, swinging through trees.

I dreamed some monkeys were climbing a vine to the sky, laughing and laughing, and one looked down to me and said, "This is the way to die." Did it mean by laughing or by climbing? I think it meant laughing was the way to die? Yes, it did.

In 1945, a case known as *The Screws Precedent* was settled in the Supreme Court. Two years earlier in Georgia, a Black man named Bobby Hall was accused of stealing a tire. Because he defended himself with his hands, he was beaten to death by the White sheriff who had a grudge against him already. He was whacked with a club for 30 minutes and dragged on his back into the courthouse where he died. The sheriff, a man named Screws, was accused of violating Hall's civil rights, and soon after was voted back into office. The Supreme Court couldn't see how Screws had the intention of violating Hall's civil rights. Someone shouted: "Whaddya mean, civil rights? He killed him." Everyone laughed. This decision established a precedent that made it difficult for federal officials to name civil rights violations as crimes.

Ordinary camouflage is sort of ghost gray, like a soft fog in a flower garden that makes every color brighter. Coyotes are scruffy and scrappy like Franciscan tunics in the 13th century.

Howl, The Invisible Man.

But camouflage, invented to cover up one lie, becomes a forest that is without a beginning or an end.

Directly after the McCarthy Hearings were over, Pa turned his attention to the Civil Rights Movement and school desegregation; to interpret (and act to realize) the aspirations of the Constitution and Fourteenth Amendment. It was already 1954, three years before we drove to Waterville, Maine. All political matters are connected if you look back now to the laws being made then, the evolution of a kind of American, the whimper of democratic ideals, and the bang of guns and bombs and wars for oil. What we couldn't see was already implied in our bleak studies of the country's literature. "Camp" is a word referring to a good-natured way of life.

But when I hear that word, I think of bunks, of snow, of guards, of orders, of frozen feet, homelessness, a kind of world Weimar with a camp tucked into its forest.

Spoken by Isaiah Berlin:

Negative liberty is the absence of obstacles, barriers, or constraints. One has negative liberty to the extent that actions are available to one in this negative sense. Positive liberty is the possibility of acting — or the fact of acting — in such a way as to take control of one's life and realize one's fundamental purposes. While negative liberty is usually attributed to individual agents, positive liberty is sometimes attributed to collectivities or to individuals considered primarily as members of given collectives.

MDeWH wrote to his sister:

Dear Helen,

My chief enterprise, of course, was the three-day session in Atlanta. I came back with a renewed and refreshed hostility to everything southern from grits to whites - everything, that is, except these impressive Negroes who go back to one evil court after another trying to prevent the indecencies from continuing. My "students" came into Atlanta from other outposts in Georgia, from Alabama, and from the Carolinas. Many of them were essentially ignorant, some of them were bright and well-trained, all of them (well, nearly all of them) were deeply impressive in their good nature and their courage. What was most shameful, of course, was the fact that they stand entirely alone in this cause - not one white lawyer in the communities in which they practice has stood with them in the civil rights cases - or if they did, here and there, they were driven out of town and out of the state. These NAACP lawyers from the north - particularly Jack Greenberg - are a very impressive group. They operate on a hit and run basis, tearing into some Mississippi court house they do a great deal to help the handful of Negro lawyers who are on hand, and then rush off to some other state to put out another fire. The months ahead are, of course, terribly grim to contemplate, but I like to think that in all other states than Miss. and Alabama the enactment of the Civil Rights Bill - unhappily, I fear, watered down by Dirksen and Bobby K. will bring a brief respite from violence and demonstration. My next involvement doesn't come until the end of July when I'm committed to do another three days of teaching in Washington - a relatively easy and unexciting assignment.

Mol is in a state of despair over Barry Goldwater's triumph. I take it in stride somehow remaining confident that LBJ won't die. If he lives it seems to me to make little difference to the fate of the nation or the universe how ridiculous the Republicans make themselves. I also have an uninformed suspicion that hatchets, knives, knuckles, and gouges will be put to work over the next few weeks to bring the elimination of Barry and the resurrection of Slippery Dick. Will that be a gain? At least it will give the nation the opportunity to give him the clobbering in November that he deserves. I've got some teaching commitments here at the Law School for money late in July and the persistent obligation to get my Weil lectures written in large part during July and August - so there'll be little if any leisure.

Pogo

Pogo was a cartoon figure born in 1948. He was an opossum with strong political opinions. He lived in the Okefenokee Swamp and was drawn by Walt Kelly. *I Go Pogo* was a best-selling book. In 1950 I took a train to New York wearing a handmade button reading "I Go Tito."

Who was Tito?

One of the post-War leaders who ran Yugoslavia and reorganized it according to his principles, which were socialist and experimental, anti-Soviet and very advanced.

But he was a Communist. Right?

When Pogo said, *We have met the enemy and he is us*, did he mean animals like him or the person (Walt Kelly) who invented him?

The other popular figure born in 1948 was the Shmoo. The already-famous Al Capp created a fat, white, and shape-shifting blob who likes to be fried in a pan and eaten. He is hard to catch, lives on air, and reproduces without sex. He was adored by half of the American public.

And I remember at that time pretending I was a Shmoo running up and down stairs on all fours and drinking out of a dish. I felt atmospheres of imminence. I looked into the middle distance and spent a lot of time waiting. I loved without being loved the way I loved. I was the dolt who would wander off and find her way home through the cracks between bricks and the lights against branches. I kept coming back!

The wait was long, too long, became longer between being picked up, dropped off, waved off, and finding a way home. Every dog we owned was my true love: Waddy, Minnie, Wendell, Candy, and Sorrow. I studied a way to look at the world through a dog's eyes: with unspeakable attention.

In the early part of the Cold War, psychological warfare blossomed. Children in school learned all about Chicken Little and death from the sky, and drew pictures of bombs and guns in the margins of their notebooks. The warrior-comic book industry flourished alongside subtler funnies. Neurotic people were called "insecure."

In the field of particle physics, "shmoo" is a high energy cosmic ray survey instrument used for the Cygnus X-3 Sky Survey at the Los Alamos National Laboratory.

Don't understand how we measure air? I think this lesson is over.

My mother kept returning to Ireland by staring east over her typewriter. She squinted and the Wicklow hills came into view.

Dear Fan:

Thanks for the reflective (or should I say demanding) letters on your summer's plans - or should I say hopes? Let me try the tough job of saying in a very general way what I think is involved.

I don't believe that you should too hastily reach a decision to abandon college. I can hear your quick response - there's been no haste - you have thought of the problem for a long time and you have decided that you don't want to get a degree. I think you know that I have never been one who insists that a daughter should be forced to complete a college course if she doesn't have any inclination to do so - and I stand by that view. I do think, however, that there's some danger that whim will take command of judgment - that your somewhat bounding spirit and restless mood will lead you to "quit" - to use an ugly word - an enterprise that becomes a little pedestrian and uninspiring.

You tend, I fear, to see that the fields on the other side of the fence in front of you are very much greener than the field you occupy. Perhaps you would do well to ask where and what you hope to be five years from now rather than where you would prefer to be six months from tomorrow. I take it that there are very few sophomores (at least in the liberal arts, so-called) who would not prefer to spend a season or a year wandering through Montmartre and Cairo to the ugly task of accumulating the tedious experience of discipline. I am not trying to say that you must - or even that you should - stay on at Stanford until you walk away with an A.B. under your belt. All that I ask is that you pause a little longer than you have in reaching what seems to be a final decision.

If I were to make my point in somewhat less offensive terms I might put it this way: I see no reason in the nature of things or in some law of morality to compel you to stay with a college for four years, I do wonder, however, whether you would not be wiser to plan a year abroad - if that seems indispensable to you - which would represent something more than an aesthetic protest against rigidities that seem offensive. If you are to be in Europe for a year would it not, in other words, be better to be affiliated with some kind of effort that would bear relationship to something other than release? To be specific, would it not be better to sign on for a year of study at some institution - such as the Syracuse school in Florence - then to aim somewhat wildly at "getting a job in Paris" - whatever that may mean beyond having a good time staring at the glories of your unfading self?

These reflections, I'm sure, seem stuffily parental, academic, and Cantabrigian. Your tragedy, however, is that it's to such a spirit that you must turn for support. I shouldn't be so pontifical and parental on the long term problems of making a life for yourself if I didn't think that your summer plans are related to these issues.

From everything that you have said in your last two letters I gather (perhaps wrongly) that your hopes for the summer are based on your plans for the future, and since I can't help asking whether those plans have been really thoughtfully worked out I can't help asking whether the summer dream is as indispensably important to you as it seems. I don't mean to say that on financial, moral, or any other grounds I'm saying NO to the possibility of your getting abroad this summer. All that I am trying to suggest is that a European trip should be planned perhaps - on somewhat different long-term aspirations than those which seem to control your judgment at the moment.

One final word and plea. We can't, I think, find a satisfactory solution to these problems by an arrangement in which you become a borrower from me, and to do so undertake all kinds of work which have no relationship to your basic commitment at the present time. In other words it seems to me absurd for you to proceed on the assumption that if you earn some money as a waitress and neglect the things you are there to do - study and write - you will have made the whole problem vanish in a cloud of gold. Of course the expense of fulfilling hopes is a factor, but it's not such a controlling factor as to justify the abandonment of other less appealing ends. I suppose that what I really am seeking to ask you is whether you have thoroughly thought through the implications of your immediate impulse. I cannot rid my mind of the feeling - I might even say the conviction - that you should be very slow to drop college - that having gone half way it may well be the wise, though not at the moment the most exciting course to stay with it - at Stanford or some other college. I should be less skeptical about your ambitious summer plan if I were satisfied that it is not simply the by-product of what may be a too hasty decision to set sail on an uncharted sea of hope.

I'm unhappily sure that nearly everything that I have said will outrage, disappoint, and infuriate you. Perhaps if you will shake aside your anger you will be able to understand that I'm not slamming the door on Europe for the summer - that may be possible. But if you are to work out a feasible plan for that particular period I want to have some confidence that it bears a rational relationship to your general scheme of things for the next two or three years. If I haven't been impossibly difficult I hope that you will patiently ask yourself whether there's not some merit in my doubts and my questions.

In any case I've done my best to say my say.

Dear Daddy:

A year after you died, I married. Did I tell you already? I had three children in four years, I don't know how or why. This is where Aunt Helen's report on me came in from New York after her visit to my house in Boston. I had the three sticky-fingered children trotting all around when my husband swooped past in a beautiful new coat — handsome, polite, intellectual, Catholic, from the South, race-obsessed, asthmatic, and a political junkie, all brain and judgment.

(I always had a dog: Woofer, Hippo, Anubis, Chubby, Dumpling, Ruby, Blue, and Ramona.)(I learned everything from dogs.)

What you would never guess is the true reason we were first interested in each other. Not race, not revenge, not sex, not rebellion. But it was conversation that bound us: his family and our own. Ideas. Books. (Africa, socialism, Lumumba, Freire, Chavez, etc.)

We could have been shot in the back, or smashed to the pavement face down, or taken off to jail, jeered at, doubted. We could have laughed ourselves to death, we could have been cruel, a wordsmith with a razor in our teeth, we could have come out of prison knowing everything and not being able to speak of it, or never gone to prison but still knowing everything and only able to laugh in secret.

Some Catholics are like this during Mass, swallowing their emotions like gum, and some women too, but on their sides in bed with the pillows over their mouths. That kind of hilarity is brought on by a spirit outraged by fraudulent humans. Or by ecstasy around the unmentionable. Hysterical laughter can be a devilish sign, when you don't want to get in more trouble, or see the teacher or priest bubbling, or listen to the male voice drone on. There is a goddess named Hilaritas who gets under your shirt. She is just too funny to be seen. Then you get kicked out of school.

To fear is an emotion never to be spoken of. To admit fear is humiliating. It's like a bit in a horse's mouth, he can't spit it out. An ironic smile is its only sign. I had an overwhelming fear that something would hurt my children, but I kept laughing at my own and their jokes and devoted my fun to them.

57

Their watchful eyes, their trembling chords. They depend on someone to understand what they are hiding in their temples. The body is a temple from which they call out the failures of God.

And then?

I will never tell.

Fan, Come on. Were there any compensations for your generation after the failures of Vietnam and your endless protests?

First came Malcolm X at the Harvard Law School Forum, a Puritan speaking of a world outside America. Then came the Supremes and Marvin Gaye and Zora Neale Hurston, Toni Morrison, Doris Lessing, and Garcia Marquez.

Compensations? Yes! Friendship, alliances across oceans, music, and an exchange of ideas in translation. I participated in protests and actions, and moved cross-country. Vietnam was prophetic. Foreign wars would fail America. I never went into jail or exile; each of my daughters did.

Hey, Pa, do you remember writing this letter (that you sent to Ma in 1936 from the battlefront of Boston Common?) It must have been summer. You had been married a year and she returned to Dublin, homesick. Your self-confidence was on low:

I really am depressed to know that I am destined for the normal obscurity and insignificance of humanity, but as the idea becomes more settled it becomes a little less irritating. All my scorn of mediocrity is only an expression of my recognition that I share it with the rest of the world. My chief effort from now on will be to bring to you as much security as I possibly can, and to let the fancy ambitions of my twenties drop back into a position of insignificance.

From Sicily:

My judicial duties began the other day - it was with considerable trembling that I ascended the bench; over my head hung a portrait of Victor Emmanuel & a crucifix. By my right hand was a bell which I timidly tinkled to preserve a tenuous sort of order in the courtroom; by my left hand was another crucifix. Thus framed by sanctity and authority the Yankee Unitarian took over the reins. I tried to glare severely at the prisoners as they were brought before me - but, as you can imagine, the terror of the accused was equalled only by the fear of the judge. The consequence was that my sentences were unbelievably mild. Already I have built up the reputation with the local populace & bar of being a soldier & jurist of unparalleled kindliness - a reputation which doubtless will soon change to an impression of unparalleled cowardice. I was told after the proceedings that to one thief whom I gave a one week's suspended sentence of imprisonment an Italian court would have meted out three years of hard labor. If there were some companion here with whom I could share the amusement & comedy of my role, life would be much more bearable - but in an atmosphere of British dignity & self-importance it's hard not to begin to see one's self as Pukah through & through. Even your antipathy - which I fully share - for the Italian people wouldn't lead you to overlook the appalling tragedy & squalor of the little frightened lives which they have been leading. The rubble of warfare is only the surface - behind the shattered front of every house lies the ancient dust of slovenliness & persecution. When some miserable thief has stolen the sandals of a British officer it's impossible for me to see his offense as very grave - but my sense of justice seems to be neither Italian nor British. I hope that fact may be of some advantage to the people. When one is informed that another defendant has nine children, of whom five are deaf-mutes, much as one would like to imprison the Archbishop one finds it scarcely a remedy to send the father to the jug. The business of judging is not, for one of my temperament, an easy one. When I sent a horrid Egyptian off for six months my stomach sank much lower than his - and it was comfortable for neither of us.

Mark DeWolfe Howe, 1943

Dear Pa,

You probably don't remember (since I had married once before) but I told you that very soon after you died, I got married again. It was only a matter of months since you died, and I was helping Ma clean out and sell the house so she could return to live in Ireland. What a riot.

Can you believe it? She was always homesick for Dublin and now, at last, she could return. You were dead. I was a drop-out and I had nowhere to live. My sister Helen was in Ireland too. Sukey was married.

Aunt Helen was, from the beginning, against my marriage, repeating that "colored" children would not be a good idea. Uncle Quincy (a left wing commentator in NYC) applauded me. And you, of course, would have given me advice as you did before.

Because, guess what? I am married, again! Only 18 months after you died. Weird.
Or did I already say that?

In 1967 the country passed the Civil Rights Act. Since our drive north in 1957, and the ten years between, the acceleration of backlash and active and very cold acts against progress, the country has changed. There is something built into our national system, self-destruction, that goes round and round; repetition without progress; evolution of disagreements. So it goes, stopping at the same stations, having the same scuffles with the same people, scratching down the same punishments and laws only to create a population of government-haters, money-makers, angry nationalists with power, and the rest wage-slaves.

There will come a day when the poor and the old will be the only manimals who know how to live on the earth. They will lie down and watch the stars and chew the fat. They will know that they can't go out of their heads because their heads are part of their bodies. Their bodies are unified entities made of a substance both science-based (atomic, hydrogen) and something unexplored and beyond marginal.

61

Are countries always at war with themselves the way people are?
Isn't that the point of law?

Some people thought an "Indian" was a White man with another, darker figure inside. "Kill the Indian, save the man." The word "colored" stood for a White person being tainted by a drop of slave blood; or was it the reverse? I can't remember now. Or I don't understand. Farm-workers, sex-workers, child porn. All these get mixed up in the blood and dust, and this is how decaying DNA can turn an anthropocene woman into a jug on the table.

David Bohm is right: Maybe the universe is a block of iced light. Premonition is the only way out of the trap of quantum history. To sense the face of yourself coming and to change your course before it does! You are coming to kill yourself. You are crossing the curve from the underworld, up.

As if in a fairy tale, three teachers told me my three flaws, the way a mother usually does. She always referred to me as "poor Effie":

Clumsy, penniless, gullible.

Why did you get married when you already knew what a serious commitment it is? Interracial marriage was only recently legalized.

So who was the fool in the case of my marriage?

I was dead. I wouldn't know. Maybe it was a tragedy, not a crime, and neither of you had the slightest idea of what you were doing. Or would soon learn.

You were dead, you will therefore always be over.

On the other side, spirits sprawl like spilled bottles but keep their tools close at hand. Hammers, knives, nails, guns, arrows, books, and pens.

Unfinished novels are the most pathetic of all leftovers.

I once knew a woman whose boyfriend beat and humiliated her. After she ran away from him, far away, she said "he was my teacher." He drove her into total independence.

The robins are back after an early Fall break. The air is hissy with crickets. Boston Harbor? Like the beach at Sandymount, Dublin.

Dust is dust and dirt is dirt.

If the nation was unable to abolish its fear of color by pretending color didn't exist, then when a person appears out of the nowhere of all our days and meetings, the spell is broken. White is blah compared with soil. The American master is the face of a people who value only what they own. An apparition is a penniless stranger arriving out of a past. The 13th amendment made all slaves free slaves. How do you allow "slaves" to have freedom and equality except among themselves; or do they stop being slaves? How do free slaves enter the world as slaves who are free?

"Hey, Pa, that slave is free."

My children's father said, Make them be Black.

I was White and he hated that.
The children were half and two quarters milk.

Make them call themselves Black, he insisted.
Okay, of course, I replied and lifted my glass of ink.

64

I used to read, avidly, a large book of quotations that we had in our house.
I was susceptible to summaries.

Fairy tales, folk tales and poems of all shapes, sizes and nationalities were piled up on half of my bed.

This heap of contradictions made me a poor student but also a seer of the connections between one thought and another.

Thoughts were my thing.

You can be mesmerized by a shadow and a blob of sunlight on wood and never notice that they are shifting.

Martin Luther, on a day of doubt, wrote, "I lost the body of a child, a child's body, the eyes of a child, and I was afraid
And went back to find it…but I can't."

In one book I wrote in the eighties, I adopted the body of an ever-moving spirit and followed her from chapter
to chapter to see what she was seeing.

I saw frost between iron rails and babies forming in clouds, wintery water and the face of George Eliot looking down.

Somewhere the scholar Franz Rosenzweig wrote that "the self has no relations, cannot enter into any, and remains ever itself.

Thus it is conscious of being eternal; its immortality amounts to an inability to die."

Angela Davis put her pistol inside her Afro and never gave up on the Manifesto: figure out how to overcome your own oppression!

Start early, even with sibling rivalry.

Marilyn Buck, in prison for life, rarely showed a moon in her poems.

When she did, was it a reverie or did she actually see it floating outside?

Law seems to limit our abilities.

I wanted to break through the bulge of time but could not, for the life of me, understand the theory of relativity.

Negative Liberties

1959

Dear Fan:

About all that I can say is that your many uncertainties are most promising and wholly healthy. How could you know at this stage just what you want or why you want it? Others before you have been hard pressed to know what their values should be, what they should show subservient respect for questionable rules of morality, and whether those who accept are happier than those who reject the prevailing standards.

I happen to be so built that I can see no other measure of morals than human happiness. This doesn't mean that any one of us will do well to make his own contentment the object of his plans. Nor does it mean that each generation and individual is wise to repudiate all that experience has taught others. Conventions have a measure of validity through the very fact that they have survived - that most people have discovered that happiness is promoted by respect for rather than defiance of the past.

One learns two things - that intellectual adventure can be exciting and that intellectual order brings some kind of personal order in its wake. I don't, of course, know at this stage and distance whether you should stay on at Stanford for an indefinite period, I'd be inclined to think that another year of more or less routine education in some American university would be a wise investment - that it would be a mistake to let a passion for travel consume all other tastes and capacities.

The passion for travel began in 1957 when I was left alone at camp in Maine. Being dropped in an unknown situation gave me two choices: first to adapt fast and join in all the sports and learn my French, and second to withdraw into my staring self. In the staring days I began my descent into being an observer and not a participant. People forgot I was there, thankfully.

Dear Daddy:

This is why I hate facts and adults. I have found out just in time: You were a middling student right up to becoming a teacher. You were reserved, you contained your anxieties in silence, you kept your eyes on politics and history, you were like me! You didn't even rise up the ranks of the Army in one swoop, but you left the Army with distinction all the same. And you made lifelong friends.

Becoming brave must have taken a conscious effort. Something you willed yourself to be. This freed the information imprinted since childhood in you. That the world is a terrifying place to be.

This morning the sun has shifted its relation to us, subtly. Many trees fell in a storm releasing fountains of light from the now-empty spaces. But the light is not harsh, not in plaintive August. The tree frogs are loud at night, but many of the birds have gone south already.

Dear Fan,

With due paternal solemnity - but with no paternalistic authority - I can't help voicing my own protest over your present plan to go it alone in the shabbier sections of New York. This protest, I might add, is my own and is in no way stimulated by the Old Lady.

It seems to me that to take this turning is folly for a number of reasons. In the first place - and most seriously - it's likely, I fear, to encourage the more trivial sides of your temperament - the side, that is, that finds satisfaction in flightiness of conduct and commitment. What you will surely find, I think, is that you will become far too dependent upon little distractions, little escapes, and thin involvements. You will almost inevitably be sitting there waiting for some escape from solitude and grasping at any straw that flutters by. There will probably build up a stream of more or less masculine "visitors" whom you will welcome not because they offer some reality of friendship, but because they will provide distraction from loneliness. So I really believe that you will strengthen your weaknesses if you set up shop wholly on your own in a world that really is debilitating and destructive.

I also can't help taking with a little seriousness the fact that today's world - and particularly a world that's geographically centered in the hot-bed of irresponsible resentment - is a physically dangerous and frightening one. I'm not saying that you are going to be murdered or raped or murdered and raped - but I am suggesting that a girl living alone in an inexpensive loft or studio in the Village is sure to feel a constant uneasiness and be subjected to pretty frequent insult and indignity. Maybe you don't mind those things - but I suspect that if you are quite alone it will not be as easy to laugh them off as it is when you have some kind of companionship.

A third factor seems to me to be poor old Woofer. Either you will have to become her slave and radically restrict your freedom or you will have to treat her with something approaching brutality. I realize that even with a room-mate, the dog will from time to time create problems and of necessity be left alone - but surely the chances of dividing the burden of responsibility will be greatly increased if you share quarters with another.

I'm pretty sure that you will see behind my protestations some impulse that I don't recognize - perhaps a Puritan's fear of happiness, or a father's instinct to govern too long. Maybe such indecencies control my judgment. But I do think there's an accompanying element of sense in what I believe. I suppose that in the end all that I can urge with any hope is that it will affect your conduct in the slightest so that you don't rush into some "available" place precipitously. In my innocence I should have supposed that perhaps one way of breaking the barrier into maturity might be to face reality.

Dear Pa,

It's a bit late to say this. You were alive when I went ahead to The Bowery with one suitcase, my Baudelaire, *Nightwood*, my death mask of Keats, and Woofer who went everywhere with me. I was ungovernable and your warnings, or scoldings, didn't stop me, and I paid the price. Those wild months were not in any way alluring, and I spent my days indoors with the dog, or walking her, and picking up editing work to do at home for the week's pay. At night I had my marvelous, wonderful, extravagant, anarchist friends to walk the streets with me and Woofer, and I always loved to dance. But the assassinating-bullets made a hole in the Book of Our Days. Oh woe!

They shot through each page, scene, leaving a little burn-circle behind. The Great Blackout, psychedelics, and despair.

I was like you when you took walks at night around Boston, but I was female and broke (as you would often be) and it was the Sixties.

In 1964 interracial marriage was allowed into a population of mixed-race children who were around for 300 years already.

Better to be the one who helps others get freedom from suffering. You don't have to be the one suffering. That helps no one.

I guess.

I was dead. I wouldn't know about your marriage. Maybe it was a tragedy, and neither of you had the slightest idea of what you already knew. Or would soon learn.

You were dead, you will therefore always be dead. We couldn't see the future.

Sometimes the hardest times are the happiest, in retrospect. Were you happy? Free?

I was alive. It was horrible.

This is how soldiers talk about war.

Now when I glimpse the islands in Massachusetts Bay they are like pieces of an imagined world that have to be navigated. You can't skip them. They are green and granite and whacked by the sea. But they are outcroppings really from the fire below, sand and stone and sea creatures, seaweed and shells and sharks. Quincy, Massachusetts can't be (but is) my bones' destiny.

At the beginning, the American colonies were torn and driven by arguments about the Church of England and religious freedom. The Puritans and the Pilgrims were two different species. One wanted to break free entirely from church hierarchies and develop a direct relationship to God. The other side wanted to stay with the English traditional church, but more freely. It's hard to remember which was which just by their names, both beginning with P.

Puritan, Protestant or Pilgrim? Do you even know the difference?

Moses came back into their vocabulary; many were terrified. Theological conversations saved them. This adventure over the sea had a higher meaning than going out to see what was there over the horizon. They had to avoid going too deep into their experience and uncertainty, or they would go mad. They had to stay at the level of Scripture. Thank God for Scripture! On the fringe of insanity where it shivers in tiny letters, sometimes even gold letters, Scripture tells the mind to go no further.

The stories from Genesis, and Psalms, and Paul, and the Gospels gave the European occupation of Massachusetts and Rhode Island a religious purpose. They went to the lower decks where the boats and people were stored. There is no Jesus-God in those dank shit-holes.

With the deep sea an inch away from their backs. There was no law down here, only inwardness and its muddy maritime flavor.

People escaping are often on fire with religion. But first they want the unlimitness of a reverie, a freedom beyond the trees and clouds. The sky is emotional in its storms and squalls. Then they hope it is a new home they are fleeing to, the real home, the source. Fugitive fear is the scariest. The battered child and woman know how bad this is. Run, run!

"We know," wrote Paul, "that the Law is spiritual; but I am carnal, sold under sin. I don't understand my own actions. For I do not do what I want, but I do the very thing that I hate."

You should see South Boston gentrified and multi-ethnic where it stands by the harbor on its way to Dorchester and Quincy. Hills and wooden houses on narrow roads and in alleys, a clay-gray beach, stones rippling under the steel pilings. A Catholic church still functional and spotty parks and bodies shoveled under sea-bracken when Whitey Bulger was around. Saint Monica, the mother of Augustine, was often seen staring out the window to the sea. The church in South Boston is named for her. Whitey had his funeral service there. From an area Southies called Malibu, Whitey drove to the other Malibu in CA where he hid out for over a decade. He hated the Kennedys for desegregating, and would have killed Teddy for supporting integration. He was a real Bostonian, "Boston Strong."

Early Americans were not the dimwits the way I and they are now, not when they were naked and discalced under the night sky, with no city lights and no marked roads. When the boats pulled into port with their cargo, they had not yet charted the rocks and rises in the sand below. Deer watched them from the high hills, and birds stood still to see. Over time more ships arrived and crew, people of many languages and accents, colors and hairstyles, women and men, and fires were lit and houses built.

And they slowly became the manimals we are today, pushing, bitching, lying, insinuating, measuring, bullying, and demanding pay for the labors of others.

Out of the woods stepped those who had always roamed the land but not marked it. They had languages of their own and handiwork to last for ages. They knew which plant was edible and which a cure. They also had care for each other and the natural life that followed them everywhere.

> But all this is the same everywhere too. Nothing new.
> Nothing new?
> My Scripture is Nature. New everyday.
> But you? — you are nature too.

"From 1842 on, the national commitment was to favor the southern slaveholder at the expense of freedom. Congress, forced by southern demands for full recognition of their constitutional rights, provided procedures by which the fugitive slave could be brought back to his owner. This legislation was followed by the fateful decision of the Supreme Court in the renowned *Dred Scott Case* in which the Court said that free Negroes — Negroes who had never been in slavery — could not be "citizens" of the states. They were outside of our society, "free" though they might be. And thus the slave was to be returned, and those Negroes who thought themselves free and were free were not the equals of other Americans. The national decision, first by Congress and second by the Court, proved in the end to favor the slave power. And though the nation had thought in its innocence that it could escape a national commitment, it found that it had made a national commitment."

"Is the civil rights movement only a part of a larger movement? How far are the American people willing to go in pressing this movement on toward radical change? A great many of the liberals, I take it, are very eager — genuinely, ardently — to find better solutions to our racial problems than we have yet been able to find. But I wonder whether that is going to be enough. Is there not, perhaps, need for a far more radical consideration of central issues in our society before we can solve this one? Of one thing I am sure, and that is that it cannot be done by law alone. The lawyer's role in this area, important as it is, will perhaps be less important from now on. That victory is within reach. But the need for the American people seems to me to be for changes which are not capable of control by lawyers, but which need the help of minds and spirits very much broader and very much more radical in their inclination than the minds of lawyers are likely to be."

What I trusted as a child, I now believe.

Really? How so?

I see that we are all born equal, not because in our infancy we weigh about the same, but — I shouldn't have to say this.

No, you shouldn't. Only a very fortunate person puzzles over equality.

Doesn't "Born equal" mean each is vital to the whole. More than value, or place? Wine?

Are we born equal before being born?

We are born out of nothing and into nothing we go.

The rabid search for blood relatives in DNA is a sign of orphanhood.

All is equal in potential.

It has nothing to do with measurement. Darwin and the influence of embryos on ancestry studies.

Was there a Judge, a woman, a man waiting? Is growing-up a metaphor for illness? Which would have come first? The action or the judgment on it? If judgment preceded action, then action would have to precede judgment... Time would be circular.
Why did I think so much over the years?
It is truly a mystery why you wanted to tell a secret to an invisible person using a rhythmic method and scores to do so.
Surely related to the composition of music, thinking is a solitary and entirely mental activity. It is the brain at work, sieving out the effects of life on the body and shaking it into an order recognizable by its likeness to the other thoughts. It has to have a rhythm for the brain to stay focused on reproducing that beat from the blood and breath coursing from ear to ear.

All we can trust now is that the things that we dominated to death will save the earth and creatures on it.

Daddy, are you deaf or something? Do you breathe thoughts from under that stone in Quincy Graveyard or from the skies around where the water folds and unfolds in bays and harbors.

Squantum and Wollaston and the approach to Boston's brown bag sand. Paupers and presidents must have shoveled their way north.

We all had our theories about what would happen after death, some bio-based, some class-based, and some incalculable. If you tried to recapitulate a life, you would find hollow spaces that ate the whole theory up.

Very stubborn children refused to give up the feeling of God — until they did anyway, give it up. Some cried inwardly for years to come at this loss and limit. Some shook themselves off and carried on as moralizing predators.

If you could hear the full murmur of those who refused to accept a world without meaning, you would feel what the ocean really weighs.

A child with very thin skin would die at the sight of an animal being hurt. Another child reassured them by stating firmly that there is a heaven for animals.

I think the people who believe in God (despite all the evidence) don't experience that belief as a mistake but as a passion of their own to see and to hear what goes past so fast.

I am sorry, Daddy, for forcing you to write humiliating reprovals to me for my failures and disappointments. I know you hated doing that, and I know your tone was already diminished, weary, and possibly leading to heart failure. Why do you always come back with your briefcase and a hat on and a look of guilt? To apologize? Is it the natural thing to do, to be sorry for dying but not guilty for it. God's policies amount to genocide after all, a mother knows this.

February 28, 1967

Mark De Wolfe Howe died early yesterday morning at the age of 60. He was stricken at his Cambridge home during the night by a coronary occlusion, and died before dawn. The snow he had shoveled lay piled on the lawn. It blew here and there into colorful dust and gems. How cold it must be in the sky, thought a little sparrow.

Howe was deeply rooted in New England. He couldn't tear himself away. He tried after college and joined Paramount Pictures as a second assistant director, working on pictures with Jimmy Durante and Fred Allen. He loved American comedy; his sister did stand-up acts; his mother Fanny was a very funny person. But he was persuaded to return to Boston and stay there.

His life until the War unfolded in predictable ways. That is, predictable for his social class and time. He read, wrote, and studied law while he was the secretary to Mr. Justice Holmes. He was, like one of his daughters would be, a passionate scholar of New England history and the characters in it. His writing style could be called poetic, it was so delicate in its thought.

He married an Irish writer and actress in 1935. Her name was Mary Manning. He went to Dublin to meet her people, and never returned. Instead he went to the War (with a Bostonian's hatred of travel and attachment to New England weather) and traveled mostly in North Africa, Sicily and Italy, Potsdam and Washington, before returning to Cambridge and his family.

From then on he worked ten hours a day in his office at Harvard Law School, and at home producing meticulous work on Holmes, New England history, religion, and engaging in local and national politics. His attention darkened. He called himself an atheist and acted like one in that he viewed humans as fully responsible for their acts. He had awakened, overseas, to the unbreakable and barely visible forces that agonize events.

During the Cold War he became active in the Army-McCarthy court battle, while advising his students on political actions, and critiquing school segregation and its effects. He had put his attention on the amendments to the Constitution and how they were used and abused, and this led to his commitment to Civil Rights.

In the USA, where slavery is foundational, he discovered in the courts little more than evasions, self-delusions, hypocrisy, violent police, red herrings, and lies on the subject of race. People love owning slaves and have created an economy to explain this.

There are 29 boxes of letters and writings by MDeWH in the Harvard Law School Library. In these boxes you can find a period in history where liberalism emerged and where it concluded, you can find personal correspondence with mighty people, and with nobodies, a historian with a Dickensian twist and style, and with an ethics only just recognizable now in poetry and some theory.

What I trusted as a child, I now believe.

Because of the mystery of repetition, I wanted to know why, when slavery formally ended, it went on, both internationally and especially in the American courts, as scapegoating.

I turned to my father's papers on law, the constitution, civil liberties and civil rights, coming to the conclusion that younger legal historians would be better at research and interpretation than I would ever be. But I still dived into his personal letters written before, during, and after WW2 to take a more experimental approach. And I am glad to report: I learned something. Hypocrisy shines through! You don't actually need to know that much to see its hideous glint inside the courtrooms.

It was like trying to do an autopsy on the unconscious, the evidence being what was not revealed. Only the flotsam around it. History. Nature. Voices. In the end I always turn back to the heartbeat of poetry — it's healthiest when it's irregular. Having grown up in the atmosphere of politics during the Cold War and real War before that, in the Red Scare, Vietnam, Civil Rights, I could still smell and taste those years and read first-hand the words with their rhythms now slightly foreign.

I had three children whom my father never met, and of course never will. They had their own six, who added up to nine among us. The three of mine self-identified as Black, and each of them could have had a different mother, but didn't. The oldest is an ex-pat and writer who left this country when she was 21. The middle child is a writer whose main subject is race. And their brother is a graphic artist who draws cartoons of Americans who are part human and part animal. Their father and I divorced seven years into the marriage and never speak to each other. None of my children married someone White, and I never married again.

Where should I start? One could, I take it, discuss civil rights problems from a number of different standpoints. It would be a defensible process to discuss the differences, as our law and our political theory have seen them, between the concept of liberty and the concept of equality. If one looks at the development of American constitutional history, he can see an always-unresolved difference between these two concepts. Another approach would, I think, be to emphasize the problem of federalism, and to suggest that the achievements and the failings, the successes and shortcomings, of this nation in the area of civil rights is very largely the product of our federalist organization of political institutions. This, I think, is perhaps at the center of this problem. In what I say this morning I shall give considerable attention to the ways in which our federalism has both frustrated the resolution of these problems and has also made the problem essentially a legal one. To say that problems of federalism have given birth to problems of law in a very peculiar and unusual way is to suggest a third way of looking at American constitutional history, a way that emphasizes the unusual and very special role which the courts have played in the development of American political institutions.

Let me say just one preliminary word with respect to this judicial role. Sometimes it seems to be assumed (and perhaps it is easier to make this assumption from outside the country than it is here) that the courts have a kind of creative responsibility for the making of constitutional principles; if there are shortcomings at this point or that point in our history in the fulfillment of constitutional promises, the failure is that of the courts. But in fairness to the judiciary one must never forget the fact that the Supreme Court's power is only the power to decide "cases and controversies" arising under the laws and the Constitution of the United States. It is, in other words, a judicial body and not a political body. As the judges conceive their role, and, I think, as those who drafted the Constitution conceived their role, it is that of passing upon constitutional questions which happen to be brought before the tribunals in the course of litigating conventional problems — conventional problems between private persons as well as problems of law that are presented when public authority is involved in litigation. Therefore, I think you must always have in mind the fact that the Judiciary does not have power suddenly to set the nation on a new course. It only has that power when the opportunity is presented in matters of litigation. The courts resolve cases and controversies, and they do not have the responsibility of deciding questions of political theory or political philosophy. Now, this interrelationship between

82

the problem of federalism which I spoke of earlier and the role of the court is, as I said, a crucial element in the story of civil rights in the United States.

Let me deal with our problems from the historical standpoint. And let me first remind you that the structure of our government as it was established in 1789 was designed to give to the federal government very restrictive authority. There were certain areas in which the experience of the 13 independent states had shown the need for coordinated action. For the resolution of those problems certain powers were conferred upon the federal government. But the objective was to set very narrow limits of federal responsibility.

Let me underline one special feature that bears very directly — at least historically — upon the problem of civil rights: the problem of the status of slavery in that society that was born in 1789. One of the most striking, and in a sense one of the most scandalous, aspects of the Constitution as it was then written was that although everyone knew that the central problem was going to be slavery, the federal Constitution didn't use the word "slavery" or face the question of what should be done about it. Ashamed of slavery, the nation was unable to abolish it, yet was unable to acknowledge that it existed. All that was said of slavery in the Constitution was that after 20 years the national government could prohibit the "slave trade with foreign nations." It was very manifestly, and I take it very tragically, an assumption of all persons involved in the creation of the nation that the Congress, the President and the federal courts must keep their hands off the problem of slavery and leave it to the resolution of the states. Massachusetts could have her abolitionists, and they would have the right to talk about abolition in Massachusetts. New England would have her right to recognize that men coming here from the South as slaves would become free if, with the consent of their owners, they chose freedom. This recognition of the right of each state to determine the condition of slaves and free Negroes had, of course, its counterpart in the South, and there was a national promise, not explicit but implied, that the nation would do nothing to abolish slavery in the South. The problem was therefore a problem of the relationship of state to state with respect to this institution, and not a problem of the relationship of the nation to this institution.

Beyond these problems of the status of slavery lay the problems of civil liberty in general. What, if anything, could the nation do about freedom, about liberty, about speech — about the institutions upon which freedom and liberty are dependent? Again, I remind you, the nation could do very,

very little. Our renowned Bill of Rights, which constitute the first eight articles by which the Constitution was amended, only set limits to what the national government could do. When the First Amendment says "Congress shall make no law respecting an establishment of religion . . . or infringing the freedom of the press," this meant quite clearly that Congress could do nothing; but it didn't say that the states could not adopt laws establishing religion and controlling the press. State authority in the area of civil liberty was virtually unlimited as far as the federal Constitution was concerned. The guarantee, in other words, was a guarantee in the Bill of Rights that Congress and the nation would not do certain things. It said nothing about what states might do to Americans.

Let me add another complicating fact to this story. That is the strange silence, again, of the federal Constitution with respect to the status of an American citizen. There is no recognition in the Constitution that there is such a thing as "United States citizenship." Every American is a citizen of the state in which he resides. But was there such a thing as American "citizenship" before the Civil War amendments were adopted? It was an unresolved question. I emphasize this to underline the fact that a man's important relationships were with his state government, not with the national government.

Let me mention one thing that did come out of this pre-Civil War period. Though the nation tried to maintain silence about the problem of slavery and sought to leave this question to be resolved by the states themselves, it became increasingly evident that this effort to evade the problem — this effort to look the other way — could not succeed. It became evident, and the courts were compelled to face this problem, that the nation must have a policy with respect to slavery even though it couldn't be found in the Constitution. What about the fugitive slave, for instance? What happens to the slave who escapes and finds his way into the North, and his owner then appears in the North and demands re-delivery of the slave? The Constitution had a provision on this, but it didn't speak of "slavery." It spoke of "fugitives from service." And it made provision for the return of such fugitives. The ways in which the courts and the nation dealt with this produced at last a decision that the Congress must deal with the question. The Congressional decision was the final decision, and if Congress said the fugitive slave must be returned, no agency could be used to frustrate that national policy.

The Civil War had its ambiguities, and these ambiguities run through the whole of American history. Was it a war for "freedom" or a war for "union"? Why was the North engaged in this war? Some northerners unquestionably fought the war to abolish slavery, for "freedom." Others, however (and perhaps this was the dominant spirit in the North) were less concerned with "freedom" than they were with "union." And one had to acknowledge, if he were to be honest with history and with law, that the Constitution did endorse the institution of slavery by its silence, and Congress by its action. How could one defend a change of law when the Constitution supported slavery? There was thus some unwillingness in the North to engage in this war for "freedom," for that was to change the constitutional structure of our society; the only legitimate cause for war was "union," to preserve the nation as a nation.

The close of the War brought three profoundly important Constitutional amendments — amendments which, certainly from the standpoint of those who had fought the war for "freedom" marked a revolutionary change. The 13th Amendment abolished slavery and involuntary servitude, and gave Congress the power to make the abolition effective. Thus the Congress, for the first time, had the power to deal with the problem of racial equality. The first thing that Congress did was to adopt a statute saying that "all persons born in the United States are citizens of the United States," thus trying to undo the damage that had been done in the Dred Scott case. It went on in the same statute to say that the Negro citizen, made a citizen by this enactment, should enjoy equality of rights with respect to contracts, the holding of land, the inheritance of land, suits in the courts of the states, and the giving of evidence.

Some persons doubted — and the President was among them — the constitutionality of this Act of 1866, and therefore it was considered advisable to adopt a further amendment to the Constitution, the 14th, which in effect made the statutory provisions of 1866 Constitutional provisions. Its opening sentence said that "all persons born in the United States are citizens of the United States." It went on to say that "no state shall abridge the privileges of citizens of the United States." Finally it said that "no person shall be deprived of life, liberty or property without due process of law, nor denied the equal protection of the laws," and that Congress might make this Constitutional assurance effective.

Now, let me call your attention — because this becomes of crucial importance a little later — to the fact that this 14th Amendment, unlike the 13th, sets limits on what the states may do. It doesn't say what you and I can do to each other. It doesn't say that I may not hold a person in slavery. It doesn't say that I may not deny persons of equality, or of life, liberty or property. It sets limits on what the states may do. And this, of course, is a revolution in the structure of federalism. But it is not, at least on its face, the establishment of a national power that governs human conduct. If, for instance, murder is committed within a particular state, can Congress deal with it because a man has been deprived of life, liberty, and property without due process of law? Can every murder in this land be made a federal offense, or is murder still a state offense? What about the racially motivated murder? Is it somehow different? Is there anything in the 14th Amendment to say that when a Negro is killed by reason of prejudice against him and his race, this is punishable by the Federal Government? Well, those are some of the problems which were presented by the 14th Amendment, which did — as I say — give Congress power to enforce these assurances of no deprivation of life, liberty, and property without due process and no denials of equality.

The third of the amendments (I'll say only a word about it) was the 15th Amendment, an amendment necessary in the eyes of the statesmen of that day if the Negro were to be given the right to vote in national or state elections without regard to race. What the 15th Amendment in essence did was to say that no person should, by reason of race, be denied the right to vote in state and national elections.

And that was the structure — the new structure of American society — after the adoption of these three amendments. What was the destiny of these new promises going to be? There was a brief and promising period in which the American courts — the federal courts — began to implement these new provisions and the Congressional statutes enacted under them. Cases of the kind I have been mentioning — lynching of Negroes by whites, other repressions of Negro citizens — were dealt with through federal prosecution. But in the 1870's — just about 10 years after the Civil War was fought — there was a political decision of major importance in Constitutional history. That was the decision that the effort to enforce southern "reconstruction" should not be done through military force, but that the government of the South should be turned back to the southerners. And living in the expectation and hope that these Constitutional amendments would be given effect, it was decided in 1876 to change the pattern of reconstruction, and leave the reconstitution of an orderly society, with no slavery and freedom prevalling, in the hands of the southern states. Not unnaturally, the Supreme Court of the United States accepted this political decision, and in a series of cases touching upon various aspects of the problem of constitutional law, the Court recognized that the South should govern itself, and that

Congressional legislation in the areas of private conduct as distinguished from public conduct would not be sustained.

Among the cases that have been put in your hands are the Civil Rights Cases, perhaps the most important of the post-war decisions in this area, involving the question of whether Congress had power to adopt a statute (which it had adopted in 1875) prohibiting racial discrimination in inns, theaters, and public carriers (railroads, etc.). The Supreme Court held in 1883 that this piece of legislation was unconstitutional — that the power of Congress under the 14th Amendment was the power to deal with "state action," not with private action. Whether or not inns or carriers discriminated was a question to be decided by the states and not by Congress. Therefore, Congress had sought to exercise powers which it did not possess when it tried to regulate these matters. Let me paranthetically point out that one of these cases involved discrimination by an interstate railroad, and remember that Congress has the power to regulate commerce among the states. Could not this legislation be regarded as valid under the "Commerce Clause" since Congress can unquestionably control the conduct of interstate carriers? But the Court said that this question was not before it in the Civil Rights Cases, because they were solely concerned with Congress' powers under the 14th Amendment.

A related decision of profound significance and effect was Plessy vs. Ferguson, in which the Supreme Court held that if a state chose by its law to require segregation in transportation facilities operating within the state it could be done — that the assurance of equal protection of the laws does not mean that there cannot be separation of American citizens one from the other as long as the facilities made available are equal. Upon this foundation there developed a whole series of southern institutions, and northern institutions as well, by which separation of Negro and White citizens were compelled. And of course, inevitably, the facilities made available to the Negro citizens were inferior, whether it was in inns, railroads or public schools. Permission to segregate became part of the institution of law.

During this whole period from 1876 on — almost a hundred years — the Congress did nothing to change the situation, partly because the Court had said that Congress could do very little. All that Congress could do under the 14th Amendment was to deal with "state action," and the South, having been given the powers of government, was using its powers skillfully, if maliciously, to keep the Negro in an inferior condition. The North (this must be said over and over again) also failed to provide the equalities which the 14th Amendment promised. Segregation was by no means isolated to the

South; it was a familiar practice in the North. And the southern unwillingness to favor any Congressional legislation was unhappily supported by northern representatives in the Congress. And thus our institutions developed in such a way as to preserve and accentuate the disparities between our White citizens and our Colored citizens.

Well, why has radical change now taken place? Perhaps one has to acknowledge that the first stimulus for change, as far as Judicial opinions are concerned at least, came from influences really not operating in the racial area. Let me remind you that the 14th Amendment, with the language that I have quoted relating to deprivations of life, liberty, and property without due process of law and prohibiting denial of the equal protection of the law, speaks not in racial language at all. It guarantees equality in all matters, apparently, and it safeguards all property and all liberty against state action. As time passed there was an increasing awareness outside the racial area that state action, repressive of liberty, might constitute a violation of the Due Process Clause. Regulations of economic activity might involve either a violation of the Due Process Clause as it applies to liberty and property, or a denial of equality. And the Supreme Court increasingly began to say that these assurances of the due process and equal protection clauses did prevent state action that would impair traditional liberties. I mentioned previously that the 1st Amendment, with its assurance of free speech, said nothing about state controls over speech. But what about the effect of the 14th Amendment? If no state can deprive persons of liberty without due process of law, can a state send you to jail for giving a political speech? May a state establish a licensing system? May the mayor of a city say there will be no speeches in this city until they are licensed by me? Well, the Supreme Court began to say in the 1920s, and said with increasing force and energy in the 1930s and 1940s, that state restrictions on liberties protected against the nation in the 1st Amendment were now secure against the states by virtue of the 14th Amendment. And therefore you found that state action affecting personal liberties and property interests were subject to judicial control. This, I remind you, was to produce a revolution in our federal system. For suddenly you find, as this process advances, that the Supreme Court is supervising all kinds of state action that deal with personal freedoms. Well, it is a natural and happy fact of human nature that if you begin in one area to safeguard human freedom through judicial decision, you are going to find that you are called upon to exercise this power for the protection of other human freedoms. And if, as I have said, the Court and the nation were beginning to show a new concern for liberty, they were necessarily beginning to show a new concern for, or at least a new involvement with, equality. And the Court gradually began to develop some new theories of "state action" as equality was effected.

Let me give you the problem that lay behind Shelley vs. Kramer, which is also one of the cases in your materials. I have noted that the 14th Amendment, when it says that no state shall deny persons equal protection of the laws, dealt with state action and that it doesn't prohibit me from my private discriminations. The nation cannot do anything about my racial or other prejudicial conduct against other persons. What if a community of landowners get together and agree that after homes have gone up they will never sell their property to Negroes? This is a private agreement by which equality is being denied. But is it a denial of equal protection of the law, or is it merely a private exclusion beyond the reach of the 14th Amendment? Well, many such agreements were entered into in communities where prejudice prevailed, and the consequence was often the exclusion of Negroes from adequate housing.

In Shelley vs. Kramer this controversy was presented: A person who had bound himself by one of these covenants had, in violation of it, agreed to sell his home to a Negro. One of neighbors then sought to prevent the performance of the sale, saying that it was in violation of the previous agreement. The action was brought into a state court to prevent the transaction from going through. The state court granted relief, saying that this was a private agreement and, though it might be built upon prejudice and might be racially motivated, was not affected by the 14th Amendment prohibitions. The court therefore forbade the Negro from occupying the land that he had bought. The Supreme Court, however, said that the state court's enforcement of the agreement constituted "state action" of the 14th Amendment, and that to enforce the private agreement by judicial decree was outlawed by the Amendment. Well, you see that a very large step forward was made when that decision was reached. These agreements may be valid as private undertakings, but they are unenforceable agreements. And when the state stands behind such agreements in one way or another, it makes the policy of the agreement the policy of the state. And if that policy of the state is racially motivated, it is outlawed by the Equal Protection Clause.

Another line of cases of very considerable importance concerned the problem of interstate transportation. Back in 1887 the Congress had adopted a statute prohibiting discrimination by public carriers. It didn't say what kind of discrimination, whether discrimination in the rates charged for shipping coal across the country or discrimination in the charges made of passengers. Not until the 1940s did the Supreme Court begin to say that this piece of legislation of 1887 outlawed racial discrimination against passengers on interstate trains. Now the Court read the statute as making unlawful any denial of equality to Negro passengers, when service was made available to white passengers. This, you will notice, had nothing to do with the 14th Amendment. It only had to do with the Commerce Clause, and under that Clause the Congress is quite free to regulate private action — my discriminations, my exclusions if I am engaged in interstate commerce. And thus in that area there was recognized for the first time a national power to deal with racial inequalities when enforced by private action; but remember that it dealt only with interstate transportation, and not with local activity.

Then came perhaps the most important of all the cases — the decision of 1954 with respect to segregation in education. As I said earlier, back in the 1880s and 1890s the Supreme Court had committed itself to the view that when a state provides equal though separate facilities to Negroes it is not violating the Equal Protection Clause. But I also suggested that experience quickly showed that the promised equality was in fact denied. And in the School Segregation Cases of 1954, the Court finally took the step that had clearly been coming for some time and held that the "separate but equal" rule was no longer acceptable doctrine, at least in the field of education. It said that to separate the races in the schools by state authority is to deny equal protection of the laws. Therefore, the Constitution of its own force prevents the continuation of segregated education.

That surely meant (and the Court was quick to say it) that segregation compelled by law, whether in education or anything else, is unconstitutional. And if a state refuses to make available public facilities to Negroes which are made available to White citizens, it has by its exclusion of the Negroes denied them equal protection of the laws. Let me call your attention to the fact that this was a decision with respect to the Constitution itself, and not a decision with respect to the Congressional power. One of the most shocking aspects of this whole story is that between 1875 and 1959 there was no Congressional legislation with respect to civil rights at all. The matter was left to unsatisfactory statutes enacted in 1870, 1871 and 1875, before either the Congress or the courts knew quite what the 14th Amendment meant. All that could be done had to be done by Judicial decisions. For how long could any nation expect the Court and the Court alone to advance the cause of human freedom and equality and dignity? Yet, this was what was happening in our society during the 1940s and 1950s. As these vast changes were at long last coming to pass, as the demand for equality became increasingly insistent, the Congress remained silent and the courts alone began to respond to the necessities of the times. And as the Supreme Court moved forward the South rebelled, not by acts of physical rebellion as much as by acts of purported legal rebellion. A whole elaborate mechanism of theory was revived in the South, a doctrine known on southern lips as "interposition." This doctrine asserts that the states may lawfully interpose their power between the individual and the nation and prevent the execution of national policy which the state condemns. Therefore in many varying ways, always obstructive, invariably (in my judgment) unlawful, the southern states sought to block the execution of the national constitutional policy. There were occasions in which the President of the United States came to the support of the federal judges. President Eisenhower and President Kennedy both sent troops into the southern states to insure the enforcement of court decrees. But I repeat, the Congress remained silent. It was largely, far too much, controlled by southern authority and power.

The story of the last few years, beginning after the School Segregation Cases, is one of mounting Negro demand and liberal demand everywhere for change. Finally Congress has begun to respond, and it has made its response effective in several different ways. If you have looked at the cases involving the Heart of Atlanta Motel, the little restaurant that sold hamburgers, and the way the Civil Rights Act of 1964 was enforced against it, you will be quite naturally surprised that Congress was trying to deal with a moral issue — a problem of equality — under the Commerce Clause. Why didn't Congress act under the 14th Amendment to insure equal protection of the laws to the Negro citizens? Why did Congress feel it was desirable in the Act of 1964 to exercise its powers under the Commerce Clause as a basis for outlawing discriminations in hotels, motels, and inns serving travellers, and discrimination in restaurants obtaining at least part of the food they sell from out-of-state sources? Why talk in those terms when we are dealing with problems of national morality? Why handle these as if they were commercial problems, when they are human problems?

Well, I think if you stop to think for a moment you will see that it was the natural and, I am sure, the wise approach. If Congress had endeavored in 1964 to deal with these problems under the Equal Protection Clause, it would still have had to confront the question of "state action." Let's say that Congress had adopted a statute saying that any restaurant is licensed

91

by the state, any hotel is licensed and supervised by the state. Therefore whatever goes on in this licensed establishment may be looked upon as "state action." What would have happened in the South would, I feel sure, have been another exercise in interposition. The southern states had made it clear that they would repeal all their statutes requiring that hotels and restaurants have licenses; you would then have private discrimination, unendorsed by the state. Therefore the Congress thought that since it has power to deal directly with any person engaging in activities affecting interstate commerce, it would exercise its power to regulate commerce as a means of prohibiting discrimination by any persons dealing with interstate travellers or handling goods that have come out of interstate commerce. And under the Act of 1964 that whole area of discrimination — in inns, restaurants, and facilities of travel — which the Congress had unsuccessfully sought to deal with in 1875 under the 14th Amendment has now been constitutionally dealt with under the Commerce Clause. Those things which Congress sought to do almost a hundred years ago have finally been accomplished with the endorsement of the Supreme Court.

Of course, this is not the end of the problem by any means. The Act of 1964 is a very limited statute. The section I have considered today, the section dealing with public accommodations, has to do only with certain types of enterprise. But it is unquestionably a very important area of national regulation, made constitutionally effective for the first time. The other area that is of great concern at this moment is the long-delayed problem of voting. By innumerable means, ingenious, unlawful and devious, the South has managed — despite the 15th Amendment — to prevent the Negro from being an equal in voting rights. Congressional power to deal with the problem is entangled in the usual problem of federalism. What Congress can do with respect to federal elections is one thing; what it can do with respect to discrimination in state elections is something very different. The Congress has not done anything like what it should have done in this area. But there are signs this year that it is at long last going to be able to deal with the problem, and for the first time the Negro citizen in the South will be permitted to participate as an equal in the processes of government. It may be that this is at the heart of our civil rights problem in the United States, and that only after voting rights are made effective can the promises that we find in the generalities of the 14th Amendment be made effective.

As I am sure you all realize, these questions are something much deeper than questions of law, and in a sense it is to talk about relatively unimportant things for me to stand here and talk about the law of civil rights. Will it amount to anything? Will our progress have been really significant if we get new concepts of "state action," declare by statute and decision that Negroes are entitled to equal service, equal voting rights, and no discrimination in education if the social system operates to preserve and advance the roots of discrimination?

Law alone cannot solve these problems. Where do we start — with education? Can we assure equality of educational opportunity? What good does this do if equal employment is denied the Negro? What good are equal education and equal employment if you do not assure equal housing? Is the problem essentially the problem of poverty? Is the equality we have promised the Negro going to come to him not because he makes this demand, but because we will recognize our responsibility to all persons — White and Colored — who in one way or another are oppressed in our society? Is the civil rights movement only a part of a larger movement? How far are the American people willing to go in pressing this movement on toward radical change? A great many of the liberals, I take it, are very eager — genuinely, ardently — to find better solutions to our racial problems than we have yet been able to find. But I wonder whether that is going to be enough. Is there not, perhaps, need for a far more radical consideration of central issues in our society before we can solve this one? Of one thing I am sure, and that is that it cannot be done by law alone. The lawyer's role in this area, important as it is, will perhaps be less important from now on. That victory is within reach. But the need for the American people seems to me to be for changes which are not capable of control by lawyers, but which need the help of minds and spirits very much broader and very much more radical in their inclination than the minds of lawyers are likely to be.

Acknowledgements

This collection borders on poetry, but it has been edited as a set of essays and letters without footnotes. My assistants in this process were Ezra Fox who has given tireless and inspired weeks of attention to putting the pieces together, and Colleen McCallion who illustrated the text with black and white drawings to supply an "atmosphere" more than a representation of content. Taylor Davis' cover and interior flags affected my thoughts about the book and the nation at the same time. I saw them before I saw the book. Askold Melnyczuk, the publisher of Arrowsmith Press, then saw the book before I did. Many, many papers of my father's opinions and lectures, his letters, written before my birth, have trailed me around my house for decades, and a trip to the Harvard Law School Library with my daughter Annlucien helped clarify the vision coming into view. Askold, Ezra, the staff, Colleen, Taylor, Linda Norton (artist and writer), and my sister Helen who made the headstone at the back of the book are co-creators of this small production. My thanks to them each and all, and to Conny Purtill for his exemplary design work on the pages as 2020 drew to a close and the days grew lighter. Accomplished 'near breath and herding wind' as *Qoheleth* puts it. With thanks to the Harvard Law School Library and Edwin Moloy who made the papers available to me, especially those concerned with Civil Rights and Civil Liberties. And many thanks to Rebecca Wingfield at the Stanford University Libraries who has watched over my archives and helped me unearth some of these letters.

Fanny Howe

Born in Buffalo, raised in Cambridge, left at age 17 for Stanford, California, dropped out, became part of her political, Beat and bi-coastal generation. Went back and forth across the country and to Ireland. Into New York City and out, married a second time and had three children, ran away with them, returned to Boston, hurried to Ireland, taught for 45 years in colleges and ended up in California at UCSD where she became professor emerita in literature. She wrote novels, essays and poetry.

Arrowsmith is named after the late William Arrowsmith, a renowned classics scholar, literary and film critic. General editor of thirty-three volumes of The Greek Tragedy in New Translations, he was also a brilliant translator of Eugenio Montale, Cesare Pavese, and others. Arrowsmith, who taught for years in Boston University's University Professors Program, championed not only the classics and the finest in contemporary literature, he was also passionate about the importance of recognizing the translator's role in bringing the original work to life in a new language.

Like the arrowsmith who turns his arrows straight and true,
a wise person makes his character straight and true.
—Buddha

Books by Arrowsmith Press

Girls by Oksana Zabuzhko
Bula Matari/Smasher of Rocks by Tom Sleigh
This Carrying Life by Maureen McLane
Cries of Animal Dying by Lawrence Ferlinghetti
Animals in Wartime by Matiop Wal
Divided Mind by George Scialabba
The Jinn by Amira El-Zein
Bergstein edited by Askold Melnyczuk
Arrow Breaking Apart by Jason Shinder
Beyond Alchemy by Daniel Berrigan
Conscience, Consequence: Reflections on Father Daniel Berrigan edited by
Askold Melnyczuk
Ric's Progress by Donald Hall
Return To The Sea by Etnairis Rivera
The Kingdom of His Will by Catherine Parnell
Eight Notes from the Blue Angel by Marjana Savka
Fifty-Two by Melissa Green
Music In—And On—The Air by Lloyd Schwartz
Magpiety by Melissa Green
Reality Hunger by William Pierce
Soundings: On The Poetry of Melissa Green edited by Sumita Chakraborty
The Corny Toys by Thomas Sayers Ellis
Black Ops by Martin Edmunds
Museum of Silence by Romeo Oriogun
City of Water by Mitch Manning
Passeggiate by Judith Baumel
Persephone Blues by Oksana Lutsyshyna
The Uncollected Delmore Schwartz edited by Ben Mazer
The Light Outside by George Kovach
The Blood of San Gennaro by Scott Harney edited by Megan Marshall
No Sign by Peter Balakian
Firebird by Kythe Heller
The Selected Poems of Oksana Zabuzhko edited by Askold Melnyczuk
The Age of Waiting by Douglas J. Penick